The Path of Becoming Whole

FROM A PAST OF BEING BROKEN...

The Path of Becoming Whole

FROM A PAST OF BEING BROKEN...

Faith Dravan

FAITH DRAVAN

I dedicate my book to my amazing husband and to all our children, I love you with all my heart...

Table of Contents

Faith Dravan

Preface

This book has taken me 21 years so far to write. I say, "so far," because I have struggled for 21 years to find the courage to tell my story and I am praying that this time is my time to finish writing it.

To bring all the facts in the forefront of my mind and my heart and put them down on paper for anyone to read is quite honestly the most frightening thing I have ever done. Please be gentle with my feelings and handle them with care.

Fear is a very debilitating thing. It can control you if you let it, you must fight hard to work through it. Fear is not of God. Fear is the thing that can get in our way and not allow us to complete the tasks and goals that we were meant to finish and achieve.

Many times, in my life over the past 21 years I have felt God calling me to write and complete this book. Off and on throughout those 21 years I have written bits and pieces of this book but always failed to finish it. I believe one reason is that fear got in my way. Throughout the past 21 years I often thought that I wasn't qualified to write, no one would care about my story because I was a nobody. I didn't have any amazing happy ending. I also believe that many of the struggles in my life hadn't even begun when I started writing this book and I had to go through them and live through them, learning and understanding why they may have happened. Not to mention how difficult and hurt I was with many outcomes of my story that I didn't expect would happen and learning to live with the facts that hurt me so deeply. I have no idea why, but I know in my heart that before I die, I must finish writing this book. I have had that sense of urgency only one other time in my life which I have written about in this book.

It's time for me to finish this book now, for the healing I know that God will bless me with, for the one person in this world that needs to read it, for the obedient child of God that I want and need to be.

I have no idea where you are in your life right now, if you are walking with God, if you have lost your way or if you have never really known him.

I am praying for each and every one of you that in some way my story will help you face the struggles and trials in your own life and in doing so that you will believe in God, that you will feel God's love and that you believe that he will guide you when you are lost, give you strength when you are weak and help you face all of the hardships in your life and believe without a shadow of a doubt that he will never leave you or forsake you.

I thank you for reading my story. I pray that in some

small way it will help you in your life and in the lives of those you love.

By the way, we are all somebody and each one of us can make a difference in this world and in the lives of those around us. All it takes is the desire to do so.

I pray it doesn't take you 21 years to do whatever God is calling you to do like it has taken me. May God fill you with his love and light your path and protect you from all darkness.

Love,

Faith

CHAPTER 1
Introduction

Isn't it amazing how lonely you can feel at times, even as you are pushing a cart in a crowded grocery store? One day I was in my local grocery store feeling lonely as I often do, and I remember looking around at the different people in the store. Some were mothers with their children, some were couples, and some were entire families shopping. I guess you don't have to be a single mother to experience feeling so alone. Loneliness comes in all shapes and sizes and isn't prejudice towards the rich or the poor, man or woman, child, or adult. My loneliness started as far back as I can remember and has continued throughout my life. I have spent many years trying to figure out why I feel so lonely. After many years of therapy, I realized the source of my loneliness. However, as I have begun writing this book, I still do not know how I will ever stop feeling lonely or if I will someday fill that loneliness with something other than the pain that lingers in my heart.

This book is written with the hope of helping each one of you that reads it to know that you are not alone. We are together, separately of course, yet we are together.

I use this font for my thoughts throughout the book.

I believe that there must be a purpose, a rhyme or reason to the pain that we go through in our lives. I do not believe it is possible to not be able to turn something that is awful into something that can be used for good.

It reminds me of a movie I saw as a young adult. It was about an orphan that brought happiness to everyone she met because she chose to see the good in people instead of the bad that was so apparent to everyone else. She saw so much good that eventually each person she got to know found the good in themselves and the good in one another. I remember when I used to be that way, long before I allowed the pain in my life to swallow me whole. I plan on finding my way back to the positive way of thinking.

I guess the best way to start my story is to tell it from the beginning...

Where did I come from? Why am I here? What is the true reason for my existence? I have asked myself these questions for as long as I can remember. Perhaps you have asked yourself the same questions...

I am about to embark on a journey of my past and present to try and figure out and prepare myself for the future.

I was born on December 23rd. My mother swears she would have given birth to me on Christmas day, but her doctor wanted to go to a Christmas party and didn't want to be bothered with delivering me on Christmas, so he induced my mother and took me early. I was brought home on Christmas day wrapped in a huge red Christmas stocking. *That was the Christmas stocking I used for many years.*

However, my mother did not come home with me because the doctors were concerned about new medical issues unrelated to the birth.

When I was born, my mother found out she had a new disease called LUPUS. The Doctors gave my mother at most a year to live. *My mother ended up living until she was 70 years of age.*

I have said my goodbyes to her many times on the edge of a hospital bed. She was so close to death the majority of my formative years. It was extremely difficult for my siblings and I growing up with a mother that was in and out of hospitals, never really knowing if she would come home or if she would die. A lot of the time when she was home, she was laid up in bed. *I have never discussed this with my siblings, and this is the first time I am putting this down on paper.*

Now that I am older, I realize how selfish I was not to think of how hard it was for her having to leave us, the pain not only her body felt, but the pain that dwelled in her heart knowing that she at any moment would leave behind all her young children. How powerless she must have felt to not be able to care for us when she was home.

The majority of my life, I thought giving birth to me caused the disease. Every time she mentioned, "When Faith was born I found out I had LUPUS".... I was flooded with an emotion that I received at a very young age, GUILT.

GUILT and I have been together for a very long time, in fact we will probably always be together...Unfortunately for myself, GUILT follows me on every road I have ever traveled, he's there at every corner I turn, and I simply don't know how to lose him.

Getting back to my mother and her illness, she always tired easily, she was short tempered and overweight. She had bruises all over her body and she smelled like what I thought death smelled like and it was all from the medicine she had to take to fight her disease. As awful as this sounds, I hated her. I didn't want her to touch me for more than one reason. First, I didn't want to catch her disease, even though I knew it wasn't contagious. Secondly, I didn't want to get close to her for fear she would die and leave me needing her so much. Little did I know that I always needed her, she was my mother.

I remember when we lived in the first house that I grew up in and we didn't have very much money. She would still find ways to buy me some paper dolls or coloring books when it wasn't my birthday or Christmas. I remember when I was little, she would make me look like a princess by putting my hair up and hand rolling curls, piling them on the top of my head so it looked like a crown. I know that hand rolling curls may not be a big deal to most but visualize huge bleeding sores on every finger with band aids trying to protect them from getting blood on my hair.

I remember one time my brother Arnold and I got into

trouble for about two or three weeks during the summer. We weren't allowed to get out of our rooms except for going to the bathroom and eating dinner. My mother would let us sneak into one another's rooms so that we could play together, and she would make us fresh popcorn in the middle of the day. Popcorn at night in our house growing up was a special treat. After a friend read the first portion of this chapter, she looked at me and said, "Now I understand why you always have to have popcorn at the movies even when you have just eaten. Popcorn reminds you of love," I cried.

It is true, I realize that popcorn is a comforting thing to me. I never realized that until writing this book. Little by little I am adding another piece to the puzzle of understanding myself. It is quite incredible the power of a mother's love. I know because I am a mother of two.

As I got older my mother and I grew further and further apart, and my younger safer years were but a faraway memory that seemed more like a dream than like reality.

My Younger Years

The best memories of my childhood all occurred in a small, single story, three-bedroom, one bathroom home. There was a big garden in the backyard (it took up most of the backyard). We grew tomatoes, cucumbers, yellow squash, zucchini, carrots, onions, corn, strawberries and probably most vegetables you can think of. We had a small plastic swing set that I loved. I can remember being about three years old and singing about God and how much he loved everyone. I would make up songs about the birds, bees, butterflies, and anything else that popped into my head, but just about every song I sang was about God.

I cannot ever remember not knowing, believing, and loving God with all of my heart.

My relationship with God started at a very young age thanks to my mom. My mom had a very close relationship with God, and she was the one who taught me to pray. Her faith was extremely strong, and I am eternally grateful that she instilled her faith in God in me. She would often tell me to pray for things at a very young age that I didn't even understand. I would pray for whatever my mom told me to pray for and I would pray hard. She used to tell me that although God hears all our prayers, he especially listens to children. I am so thankful for those memories. They are the most important memories I have of my mom.

The fond memories I have of my dad were when we lived in this house. He used to water the garden and I used to stay next to him singing to him all the while. I stayed outside for hours singing love songs that I made up especially for him. I followed him everywhere he went just so I could be near him. I know that most little girls love their daddy, and I loved mine too.

I was the youngest of three when we lived in this house. My brother Tommy was the oldest. He was 4 ½ years older than me and my brother Arnold was only 18 months older than I was.

My earliest memory was when I was about 2 years old. I was on a little red tricycle minding my own business when I looked down at the ground and saw a snail for the very first time, you can imagine my delight, that is until Tommy who was about 6 or 7 years old, shoved me into the rose bushes and all I can remember was my whole body feeling like there were needles in me. To this day, I remember every moment of this memory. In fact, I remember the pain as my mother pulled out all of the thorns that covered my face and the rest of my body. I also remember my father yelling, "Where is Tommy!" In my later years I found out that Tommy, like the rest of us, learned what a beating was at a very young age.

I remember one year on my birthday, (I had to be about

5 or 6 years old), it was pouring rain outside (my birthday is 2 days before Christmas) and my two brothers and I were sitting in the back seat of our green Buick station wagon. Of course, my brother Tommy couldn't sit still for long before he got into mischief. Somehow, I always seemed to be the focal point of his great ideas. Someone had handed down this royal blue, furry coat with big gold buttons to me and I was so excited because my mom had just given it to me that morning to wear. To say the least I was rather proud of my beautiful royal blue coat and in fact I remember singing about it as I was sitting in between my two big brothers. We were waiting for our parents while they were in the pharmacy shopping for Christmas presents for us (They had small gifts and games in the pharmacy).

Suddenly, my brother Tommy stood up and leaned into the front of the car. I couldn't see what he was doing because my view was blocked by his back side as he was leaning over in front of me. All I know is that it happened so fast that he didn't even quite know what happened himself. Back in the day, there were cigarette lighters in the cars and apparently my brother wanted to experiment with one to see what it could do.

My brother had taken the cigarette lighter and put the hot side down on the arm of my furry royal blue coat with gold buttons and after it sizzled, he turned the cigarette lighter over to expose gobs of royal blue fur stuck to the lighter. I think we both looked down at the same time to see what happened to my coat. It was the first time I ever saw burlap. There was a huge bald spot, (the size of a large cigarette lighter) on the arm of my coat. That bald spot bothered me for the remainder of the years I wore it. Of course, I never knew it would make me laugh so hard as I reminded my brother many years later when we were both adults with our own children. It is funny that my brother does not recollect this story, but I guess if he had to wear a furry blue coat with a huge bald spot on the arm for years it may have stood out more in his memory.

He didn't remember telling me to get small like a ball so that he could throw me across the kitchen to see if he could throw me into the sink, either. Of course, I didn't land inside the sink, but my knees hit the outside of the sink and I fell back and hit my head and got the wind knocked out of me.

Why I obeyed all the stupid things he told me to do, I will never know. My big brother was the king of, "horse play," as our mom used to call it. He could never sit still without coming up with some creative ideas that usually involved me.

Tommy has been my hero ever since I can remember. He used to do handstands with me in the living room, even after he was in high school. His long legs would look like long branches ready to collapse on me, but I didn't care because he was spending time with me, and I adored him. I hated it when he started dating. I hated all the girls he brought over to our house because they took time away that he could have been spending with me. In my older years before he moved out on his own, he was my buddy, and I was his. I remember falling in love with "The Beatles," because Tommy loved "The Beatles."

I memorized all the songs because my brother had all their albums on vinyl. Sometimes he would let me hang out in his room and he would play his Beatles albums and we would both sing to all the songs. Just the other day we were in my car driving somewhere and I had my CD of "The Beatles" and I played it, and it was like old times as we sang to all of the songs and danced in the car. It was a beautiful day outside with the sun shining in the middle of a warm August day. Even more beautiful than the day outside was the feeling of love that I held for my brother and the recognition of the precious moments he and I were sharing. Ever since I was young, I knew for some reason that I was on borrowed time with Tommy, perhaps it was intuition, or perhaps I knew from a very young age that when you love someone a lot, for one reason or another they get torn away from you. Now that I am an adult, I realize that I have had abandonment issues my entire life that stem from my mother being ill and leaving for months at a time to go to the Mayo Clinic in Minnesota or to hospitals that did not allow small children to visit. As I got older, I learned to leave people before they left me, even when I didn't want to leave because I was going to do the leaving.

CHAPTER 3

My First Miracle

When I was about 9 years old and we had first moved into our new house for some reason or another, my father stopped talking to me. He wouldn't even acknowledge me. He acted as if I wasn't there. Thinking back, I realize that I was way too young to realize what a blessing it was for me. However, at 9 years old, I was devastated that he wouldn't speak to me. I have no idea what I had done to upset him or if I had done anything at all. All that I know was that my heart hurt very much, and I learned from a very young age through my own experience as a child that the power of prayer is very strong and that miracles can come from them. This is the first miracle that I remember ever happening to me... It was summer and my father hadn't spoken to me for a month. The only time I could be out of my room was to go to the bathroom and eat my meals for the day.

I remember after I ate dinner one night and was back up in my room that it was still light outside. I got on my knees in the middle of my room and prayed for hours begging God to please let my dad talk to me again. I begged, I pleaded, and I was crying and praying out loud to him. I remember not knowing how I knew but that

I needed to ask God to make me really sick. So, I did. I started praying over and over for God to make me really ill, so ill that I almost died so that my father would talk to me. The next thing I knew, I could hardly see but I could feel my mom and dad pouring all kinds of rubbing alcohol all over me. Apparently, I had an extremely high fever that they couldn't get down. That was the last moment I remember but I later found out that they had to take me to the emergency room in the middle of the night and that I had almost died from the high fever. They never told me what I had or how I got sick, but I already knew. I learned at the age of 9 to be very careful what you pray for because when your faith is as strong as a child's you can make miracles happen.

Throughout my life, I have had God put many thoughts in my mind and in my heart, now I realize that the little voice I hear in my head is God speaking to me. God speaks to all of us. A lot of times we do not pay attention to hear him and the signs that he places in our lives for us we fail to see, and we are too busy to listen.

I pray that anyone that is reading this book takes the time to find the miracles and signs that God is trying to show you in your life.

CHAPTER 4

Out of Place

When I was younger my skin was darker because I am hispanic and I loved being outdoors. I was a tomboy at heart, I loved playing baseball, kickball, basketball, anything that was outdoors. *It's odd that I loved the outdoors so much and now I am so introverted that it is sometimes difficult for me to leave the house.* My passions were gymnastics and dancing. In between all the chores I had to do I would try to sneak outside to play baseball with my brothers and the neighborhood boys, but after a few minutes my mother would realize I wasn't working on the house cleaning and she would yell at the top of her lungs for me to get back in the house, "Faith!" *Like it was a bad word. To this day I hate my name because when anyone says my name, I relive my parent's anger towards me and the lack of love.*

I was about 9 or 10 years old when we moved to a different city the summer before 5th grade. We moved from a lower income area that was mostly Hispanics to an all-white high-income area. *For those of you that may be getting the wrong idea that I am racist against other nationalities that are not my own, let me clear this*

up right away. I love all races and ethnic backgrounds. I
do not want to offend anyone, and I am only mentioning
this because it applies to my story. Most of the kids at the
new school I went to already grew up with their friends
from at least kindergarten, so there wasn't really a place
for me to fit in. I tried to fit in and to feel like I belonged,
but there were too many things against me. I was
extremely skinny, I was Hispanic, I was awkward and sad.
I got teased without mercy. I was Hispanic in a mostly
white school. The kids were ruthless and mean. I never
met such mean kids. The kids I used to go to school
within my old neighborhood were nothing like these
kids. I already felt very alone due to my mom's health
situation. I think I started isolating myself even more
once we moved because my mom seemed to get worse,
and she was in the hospital more frequently. When
we moved, I got extremely shy. I got so embarrassed
that if I was talking to one person and another person
walked up that I would feel so uncomfortable that I
would start stuttering and eventually just stop talking. I
always felt like I had nothing important to say and that I
was nothing. My negative thoughts about myself were
cultivated for me at a very young age by my father. A
very common phrase they said to me in my house was
"Faith, you lazy good for nothing."

The funny thing was I wasn't lazy. I did more housework
than most grown adults at a very young age. I learned
how to cook and clean and actively did both every day.
My parents rarely let me go anywhere or do anything
fun. My purpose was apparent to anyone and everyone
that ever came to our house.

For as long as I can remember all I did was clean, scrub floors by hand, vacuum the stairs by hand, dust everything, clean all three bathrooms and the never-ending dishes I had to wash. Even on school nights I would be up until midnight sometimes trying to finish washing, drying, and cleaning the whole kitchen by myself. Cleaning came first. I never did homework; my grades were awful, and no one would care until the D and F notices came in the mail and then I would get punished but I would still not get any time to do my homework. I was just a child and yet I was far older in my mind than anyone would ever find out until now. My parents would rarely let me spend the night or go over to anyone else's house. *Not that I had very many opportunities to want to do that.* The very few friends I ever made never stayed friends with me for very long because they would come over to my house and watch me clean. *Even if I had a friend over, I still had to do all the constant cleaning and working and caring for my younger sister.* They made it impossible for me to ever just be a kid. I didn't realize until the last couple of years because the few friends I made wouldn't be friends with me after they came over to my house. I guess I got used to the yelling, screaming, and cussing my parents (especially my father) did to my brothers and me. The house I lived in was filled with anger, pain and evil. It wasn't the house that was evil but the people that lived inside.

My parents would not let me shave my legs even though I had dark, hairy legs. I begged them, I pleaded with them, I prayed a thousand and one prayers for God to make them let me. About a year ago, I ran across some

papers and found page after page of my handwriting
tucked away in an envelope addressed to God. Of course,
I opened it and read the same phrase over and over:
"Please God, please make them let me shave my legs."
I would like to say my writing was from when I was in
junior high school, but I remember being 15 years old
and my family had gone camping with the family of a
girl that my eldest brother was dating. She was 14 years
old and younger than me. She was shaving her legs in
the bathroom and not doing a very good job I guess, so
my mother was helping her and giving her tips on how
not to cut her legs.

As I watched my mother with this girl, I tried to hold
back my tears because I was a year older than this
girl and forbidden to shave my legs. *I was already
teased, made fun of, and mercilessly ridiculed at school.*
My hairy legs were just more ammunition for them to
humiliate me.

Later, I asked my mother why I wasn't allowed to
shave my legs when she was teaching someone else's
daughter that was younger than I was. I was told that
she was more mature than I was. My parents made me
wear the ugliest clothes and purchased all my clothes at
Kmart. *To this day, I hate Kmart.* I never dressed in style;
in fact, it was just the opposite. They bought me clothes
that were two sizes too big and ugly. They never let me
pick any of my clothes. I wasn't allowed to wear any kind
of makeup or shave my legs, even being a senior in high
school. I didn't shave my legs until the day I moved out
of that house, and I was 18 years old.

People laughed and made fun of me. I weighed about

85 pounds my senior year (I tried to gain weight, but I could never gain an ounce no matter what or how much I ate). I was in and out of hospitals since I was young for problems with my stomach, but the doctors would just admit me into the hospital and never figure out what was wrong with me. When the pain would finally go away then they would send me home. Sometimes it was days and sometimes it was weeks. I didn't start my period until I was over 17 1/2 years old and a senior in high school. I didn't even know how to use a tampon. When I finally started my period during my senior year, my mother's Avon lady's daughter had to come into my bathroom stall to show me how to use it. I was more than mortified by the situation, but I was so lucky that this girl was confident in who she was and was kind enough to help me. This girl who helped me was two years younger than I was. By then, all I cared about was God, my little sister, writing and dancing and in that order. I had to sneak to wear makeup and I had to sneak to borrow clothes from the little girl across the street who felt sorry for me. I would change my clothes at her house every morning before we went to the bus stop. I hated my life and I hated both of my parents for many years until I learned to forgive them.

I was always an outsider, at school, at the bus stop, at Catechism, (Sunday school), and in my family at home. I was always a freak; I was always different than everyone else around me. I never really had a best friend in the true sense of the word. I was pretty much always alone whether there were people around me in a crowded place or if I was alone. I learned to get used to it, I guess.

Do you ever really get used to being alone? I guess some of us pretend to even like it. To make matters worse, the kids that lived near me and went to my school didn't like hispanics. I was homely, shy, lonely and I was a Mexican. The kids at the bus stop used to call me Beaner. I have to say, that word still makes me sick to my stomach. There was a boy named Donavan who was especially mean to me. He used to beat me up and call me the meanest names in front of everyone and everyone would laugh and help him terrorize me. I don't know why, but I was always kind to him anyway. I would go out of my way to say hi to him, but he would still be mean. One day it was getting closer to Christmas and my mom, and I were out Christmas shopping. I told her I had a great friend and that I wanted to get her a nice present (I bought some candy and a stuffed animal). It was really Donavan I got the gifts for. I figured if I was kind to him and showed him kindness, he would stop being so mean. It worked for one day, the day I gave him the Christmas present. I guess I never learned my lesson from that time so long ago, because I constantly do things like that to people who are not very nice. I guess I have hopes that they will change when they realize someone notices them and cares. I have to say that there have been many Donavan's in my life that I have come across and my kindness towards some of them did make a difference. I believe that giving kindness to those who are unkind is a gift. A gift that the unkind truly need to receive. You never can tell when someone is hurting so much that they don't even realize how unkind they are until someone gently reminds them what kindness feels like.

Every night as a child and in my twenties, I used to tell
God that I forgave Donavan for hurting me so much,
because I didn't want Donavan's being mean to me
prevent him from ever going to heaven. You can say that
I was obsessed with praying that prayer almost as if I
knew that he would die early.

I went to my 10-year high school reunion and found
out Donavan was killed right after high school in a car
accident. Apparently, he was sitting in the back of the
bed of a truck when it collided with another vehicle, the
truck flipped over, and Donavan died instantly. You can
imagine my shock when I found that out.

CHAPTER 5

My Little Sister

My parents adopted a baby girl from Mexico when I was almost 13 years old. My brother Arnold was 14 and my brother Tommy was 17 years old. I wanted a baby sister so badly. When Sofia was born, I not only got a new baby sister, but I experienced what it was like to have my own child. One week after my mother brought my sister home from Mexico, my mother and father decided to go to Texas because my mother's grandmother died. I had no idea what that meant for me, but I soon found out. They left my newborn sister with me to care for. They left Sofia and I with one of my father's younger sisters. The aunt we were left with had a newborn baby of her own and her baby was the same age as my sister. To say the least I cared for my sister in every way possible. My aunt couldn't help me with my sister because she was taking care of her own newborn baby, her husband and three other small children.

I was up with my newborn sister all night long. I fed her, I bathed her, I rocked her, I held her, and I cried with her for two whole weeks while my parents were away. I had just turned 13 years old. When my mother returned from her trip to Texas she continued to go in and out of hospitals leaving me to be caretaker and mother of my newborn sister. I didn't mind because I finally had someone to receive all the love I had to share and someone to give love back to me.

Sofia started calling me mommy at the age of two. I was fifteen years old by then. I did everything for her whether my mother was home or not. My days as a child were long gone, in fact they pretty much ended when I was about nine or ten years old. My mother would get very angry at Sofia if she heard her call me mommy, so I had to correct her every time she called me mommy because I didn't want her to get in trouble. I would say, "You need to call me Sissy." But she would still call me mommy because I spent the most time with her and I did everything for her until she was 5 years old. For some reason, when she was little, she didn't tell our mother emotional things, she always told me, and my mother would get extremely angry at her and at me.

My sister has had a mind of her own since she was born. She did things at such an early age that didn't make any sense. We could never leave her alone unattended even in her crib. We had to constantly check to make sure she was asleep during her nap time because if she woke up without us knowing it, she would take off all her clothes after pooping in her diaper and play with her poop. As disgusting as it sounds, she would decorate the bedroom wall with it, put it in her hair and on her face. Our whole room smelled of poop. I was the lucky one who had to scrub her wall meanwhile removing the little if any wallpaper that was left on her wall. I had to soak and scrub her in the tub to remove all the chunks of poop out of her hair. I was a little girl myself, or so I was supposed to be behind the apron and dirty dishes. I do not understand, nor do I believe in any of my parent's upbringing. Nonetheless, they helped me to build a loving relationship with Sofia.

Sofia was the first love of my life. I remember the night before my 18th birthday, I snuck her into my room and picked her up and put her on top of my dresser. I told her I was leaving and that I was not coming back because I wasn't happy. She cried and begged me not to leave her. We both cried for a long time that night as we said our goodbyes. I told her that one day I would come back for her and one day, I did. I never wanted to leave her, but I had to leave to save my life and my sanity.

I tucked my little sister into bed for the last time.

When I was back in my room, Damian came knocking on my door. I was scared but he just handed me a little box and told me to open it. I told him that I could not accept it and he started yelling at me. I opened the box even though I didn't want any gifts from him. Inside the box there was a gold ring with rubies and diamonds in it. I told him I could not keep it and he asked me why. I told him that I was moving out the next day on my birthday. He told me that it was a gift and that it was mine and stormed out of my room. That was the last night I ever had to worry that he would come into my room to sexually abuse me.

The next day was my 18th birthday, I left with a few clothes, my new ring and my blanket and purse. As I went to go say goodbye to my little sister my parents grabbed her and put her downstairs in the family room with the sliding door closed so I couldn't see her. They told me that I would never see her again (They knew how much I loved her). They forbid me to ever see any friends of the family or any family members from either side of the family. They told me that I was no longer their daughter and that I would forever be dead to them, and I was dead to them.

Just before I walked out the door, my five-year-old little sister snuck open the door crying, "I love you sissy!" "Don't leave me!" I cried and told her I loved her and tried to hug her, but Damian and Martha blocked me and all I remember was my little sister crying and begging me not to leave her. I was crying as I was walking out the front door, finally free, all I could hear was the sound of my little sister crying and yelling, "SISSY, SISSY!" *I wrote this part of my book many years ago and just now as I am retyping it, the memory is so vivid that tears are running down my face.* To leave my sister/daughter in that house for my own survival still haunts me today. My sister is a grown mother of seven children and knowing I had to leave her behind still breaks my heart.

My friend Joey from one of my jobs picked me up that day in a tiny sports car with only two seats. I carried everything I owned at that time on my lap. I continued to cry as we drove away. I was tortured by the memory of my sister's cries as I am now at this very moment of writing and remembering it. I had forgotten how painful it was. So much pain in my heart and in my memory and I have been so good at keeping it at a distance and not thinking about such things that flood me with so much pain and grief. Although it was painful for me to leave my sister, (*something I don't know if I will ever recover from*) I was finally free from the beatings, the cussing, the put downs, all the physical, emotional, and sexual abuse. You may wonder why I didn't tell someone about the abuse, especially because I left my little sister behind. You need to understand that Damian (My father) brainwashed me. He told me since I was very little that if I ever told my mom about what he was doing to me, she would get so sick from her disease it would kill her and that he would kill himself.

When I was 13 years old it was one of the many times that my mom was in the Hospital, both of my brothers were on a camping trip, and I was watching my newborn sister alone at our house. It was about 2:00 am and my sister and I couldn't sleep because we were scared. I had her in my bed with me because we were hearing all kinds of scary sounds; walking and talking in the hallway outside our room and no one was home. I finally heard the key in the front door, so I put my sister back in her crib and ran to the top of the stairs as my drunken father came stumbling into the house. I was so angry at that moment that I yelled at him, "I am telling mom!" He ran up the stairs so fast that I didn't see what was coming next. He punched me and I fell to the ground. The last thing I remember was that he was kicking me in the head with his steel toed work shoes. When I woke up, I could hardly see, and I could barely stand. He was sitting on the edge of his bed with a loaded gun to his head. I literally crawled from the top of the stairs to where he was at the end of the bed. I begged him for a long time to put the gun down. I realized that my father thought that when I yelled at the top of the stairs down to him that I was telling my mom, he thought that I meant that I was going to tell my mom about all the horrible things he was doing to me. When I said, I was telling my mom, I meant that I was telling her that he stayed out until 2:00am and came home drunk when I was home alone caring for my sister.

When I realized what he thought I meant, I said that I wouldn't tell anyone and I physically took the loaded gun out of his hand that he held against his head.

That night will never be forgotten no matter how hard I try to forget it. The damage that night did to me I cannot even put into words. It haunts me still.

Damian continually told me what a horrible person I was and constantly made me go to confession for being such a horrible person and making him do such horrible things to me. You see, he brainwashed me to believe that I was evil and that it was my fault. I never in a million years thought my little sister was in any danger because Damian convinced me that I was the bad one. Not until I was a grown mother of two children and ten years of therapy did, I finally believe that it wasn't my fault, and that Damian was the responsible one.

Just writing that is making me break down and cry right now. If you are reading this and you have been abused by someone, I am telling you that you are not to blame. The person or people that abused you are to blame. You are innocent and they are guilty. I want you to know that you are not alone. I feel your pain.

Please find the right person to tell and get help.

Many years ago, probably when I was in my thirties and after my grandpa had passed away, my grandma told me about a day when she and my grandfather went out with my parents and my little sister.
My grandparents were alone for a moment with my sister in the backseat of my parents' car and my grandfather asked my five-year-old sister where I was. My little sister replied, "My Sissy is dead."
My grandmother told me that my grandfather got so angry at my little sister and yelled at her telling her that I was NOT dead! My grandmother told me that she never saw my grandfather so angry. I have no idea what happened next, but I know that it was important for my grandma that I knew that.

I can't imagine telling a five-year-old such a horrible lie. But then, I can't imagine how anyone could do the horrible things my father did.

CHAPTER 6

Moving Out

I moved in with my best friend and her family at the beginning of the second semester of my senior year of high school. My best friend Jane had five siblings. Four of the siblings were grown and the only one younger sibling was still in high school. Her mom was recently divorced and a stay-at-home mom.

I don't think I mentioned that when I was 17 years old my father said that I was only good at cooking and cleaning and that school was a waste of time for me, so he had my mother pull me out of school. So, moving in with Jane meant that I got to go back to school, at least for a short time.

I had a crush on the campus supervisor of the high school that I went to, and he had a crush on me as well. We had started seeing one another and by this time, he was my secret boyfriend. He was my very first boyfriend, because I was never allowed to date when I lived at home. I need to point out that by the time he was my boyfriend I was already 18 years old.

He would come and pick me up after he got done working at the school and we would go and eat or go back to where he rented a room at a condo and

watch TV. In retrospect I can see how selfish I was
by not spending as much time with my best friend. I
didn't have a driver's license and I had no car or money,
and Jane's family took me in, fed me and put a roof
over my head.

I remember the first week of the second quarter of my
senior year. Jane and I both had a psychology class. I will
never forget it because I had to have a baby photo and
bring it to class. I didn't have any baby photos, or for that
matter any pictures of myself. I remember trying to hold
back the tears in my eyes during class.

Within a couple of days, or it could have been the same
evening (it was so long ago that I don't know for sure)
I came home one evening from Ned's house and Jane
was crying on her bed with her mom sitting beside
her comforting her. I was really concerned about what
was wrong, but I soon realized they were talking about
me. When I walked into the room, I didn't even have a
moment to say a word because Jane's mom told me
what a horrible person I was and that I had to move out
as soon as I found all of Jane's baby pictures.
They accused me of being jealous of Jane because she
had baby pictures and I didn't have any. They said that
I must have thrown them all away. I was so confused
that I didn't fully understand what was happening. Why
would anyone ever do such a horrible thing and how in
the world could my best friend and her mother think
that I would do such an awful thing?
Before I moved into Jane's house, we carried a bunch
of boxes of her stuff and put it in her garage because

she was making room for me to move into her room. We carried the boxes of Jane's things out the front door and into the garage from her driveway. Apparently, she found a baby picture on the driveway, and I guess that's how they concluded that I took them and threw them away (They later found all of Jane's pictures in the garage).

I was devastated. I couldn't believe that this was happening to me. I remember looking for the box of her baby pictures in her dark garage which seemed like forever but there was so much stuff packed in their garage and it was so cold, dirty, and filled with cobwebs and spiders. I came back to the house and her mom was so mean to me. I told her that I couldn't find them, and she yelled at me to leave their house. I had nowhere to go and only one person that I could call but he wasn't home because he had just recently dropped me off at their house and he lived at least 30 minutes away (There were no cell phones back then). I remember I ran out the door with my purse and a small blanket that I had since I was young. I was crying so hard that I could barely see. It was pouring rain outside and I was like a crazy person running down the street. I knew my boyfriend had a friend that lived a few blocks away in a condo nearby. I have no idea how in the world I found his condo because I had only been there once, and they all looked the same to me.

Once I actually found the right condo that his friend lived in, I tried to tell him what had happened, but I was crying so hard that he couldn't understand me, and I just stood there crying like a baby. I guess he realized that he needed to drive me to Ned's house because that is what he did, and I cried out loud like a baby the entire way to Ned's house.

My father had forbidden me to contact anyone they knew, any family or friends of the family. I was such an obedient daughter whether they realized it or not. I had no one besides Ned to turn to. I had no other place to go. As I have mentioned before, Ned worked at my school. He was a substitute teacher now at the high school I went to and a football coach. Once Ned took me in, I couldn't continue going to school because he would have gotten fired. I had no choice at the time but to drop out of school. I only had less than a semester left to graduate high school but there was no other way. I had no car, and I did not have a driver's license. I had a job on the weekends as a hostess at a coffee shop that I worked at on the weekends, but we lived too far away from anywhere for me to even get another job since I didn't have a car.

Years later, when I was about 22 years old, after I worked my full-time day job, I went to night school and instead of taking my GED, I took all the classes that I missed in my last semester of high school, and I got straight A's in every class. I finally graduated high school, but this time I really did it for me and so that my future children would see that with determination, anything is possible. I realize how different it was to finally do something for myself and the outcome helped me to gain more confidence in myself.

The time at Ned's rented room at the condo seemed like it lasted forever. I wasn't allowed to go into the other part of the condo. I only stayed in his room because the lady he rented his room from didn't allow it. I was like a lonely hostage all alone all week until he got home at night. When he finally had time, he helped me to find a car that I could afford to buy so that I could get another job and drive myself to the job I already had. I had $1600 I had saved up in my bank account from the time I was born to spend on a car. I finally bought a beat up bright yellow VW Bug. It was very beat up and used to break down all the time, but I loved it because it was the first bit of freedom that I ever had.

Ned and I got along okay for a while but eventually he started beating me. He was extremely jealous. They say when someone is jealous it's because they are the ones doing the cheating. In my case, that was accurate, but I didn't find out for at least a year. We finally moved out of the condo we were living in and moved closer to where Ned worked. He got a permanent teaching job at another high school, so we were able to move into a studio apartment. There was only one small bathroom and a small kitchen and the room that was a living room by day and by night we turned the couch into a bed. I have never seen so many cockroaches in my entire life. In fact, at that point in my life I don't know if I ever saw any.

We got engaged when I was only 19 years old. I wanted so badly to get married and have kids of my own to love. The way Ned asked me to marry him was not at all what I had dreamed about since I was a little girl.

We were sitting on the couch one afternoon and he threw a diamond ring at me.

I picked it up and asked him if it was an engagement ring and he said yes. That was my very unromantic first proposal if you can even call it a proposal.

Ned handled all of our money. I signed over both of my checks to him each time I got paid from both of my jobs. He would only give me enough money to buy groceries and to get gas. I had absolutely no money of my own, nor did I have any access to any. I had no bank accounts and no credit cards.

My boyfriend was a big professional bodybuilder and took steroids, in fact, he even sold them. I was so naive that I didn't know that what he was doing was wrong and I certainly didn't know that they were illegal. What I also didn't know is that the steroids he was taking were making him very mean. He used to beat me regularly and I would have black eyes and bruises and cuts all over my body. One time he hit me so hard in the face that he knocked me out and left the apartment. I woke up that time from our puppy (a yellow lab) licking my face. I was in so much pain and my eyes hurt really bad. I got up from the ground and crawled to the bathroom and pulled myself up by holding on to the sink. When I looked into the mirror all I saw was blood coming out of my eyes.

Ned's jealousy got so bad that he would have his body building friends come to my work and watch and see if I spoke to any guys. When I got home from work, he would beat me and tell me that his friends saw me talking to guys. I worked at a Hallmark store and often had to be at the register helping anyone that came to the register whether they were male or female.

When I went to the grocery store to get groceries to make dinner, he would time me and if I took longer than he thought I should take he would start hitting me as soon as I walked through the door. I was scared out of my mind, and I was always in a hurry for fear of taking too long. I was extremely shy and would hardly even talk to anyone because I was scared too. I didn't have any friends. Ned would not allow me to have any. He would take off and leave me all alone for the weekend and not tell me who he was going with or where he was going, and he never told me when he was coming back. We lived in the worst area in the city we lived in and back then there was a guy named Richard Ramirez that was all over the news because he was raping women all over the state. I was scared to death.

You are probably wondering by now, "Why in the world didn't you leave this guy?" Honestly, I really don't know. I guess I was used to being beat up and at the age of 18 and 19 years old I was in love with him. He had already isolated me from anyone and everyone I knew. He made it so that he was the only person that was in my life, and I was extremely dependent on him, emotionally, physically, and financially. Honestly, I don't think the thought ever entered my mind to leave him. I believe that is why God had him leave me. I honestly think he would have killed me if he hadn't broken up with me and made me leave his house one night. It all happened one weekend.

I guess, when you have absolutely no self esteem and no one loves you even your parents, you allow others to do bad things to you and treat you in a way that no one deserves to be treated because that is all you know, and you start believing that you actually deserve to be treated that way.

We had just planned on moving to another city in a nice condo that was for rent. There was a bidding war over renting it. I went to speak to the owners along with a lot of other people that were interested in renting it while Ned was away in Vegas with a bunch of his friends one weekend.
The owners of the property agreed to rent it to me because for some reason they liked me and liked the idea of an engaged couple living there.

During that same weekend Ned was gone, Jane and her friend came by our apartment. I have no idea how she knew where we lived but I was happy to see her. Neither of us ever mentioned the last incident at her mom's house.

When Ned returned on that Sunday night, I knew something had changed in him. He was colder than normal, and he flat out told me that he had a great time in Vegas and that he had cheated on me the whole weekend. He said it almost as if he was laughing at me. He then told me that he didn't miss me, and he didn't want to marry me anymore. He told me to give him back the ring so that he could buy his buddies some cheap watches. So, I gave him back the ring, packed up the little bit that I had into my small beat-up car as I cried as if someone was killing me. In a way, he was killing me, the insides of me this time.

I believe that it was at this point in my life when I started putting huge invisible walls up around myself to protect me from ever allowing anyone to get too close to me so that I could avoid getting hurt again. I felt like God forgot about me but later I realized that God saved me. *You may be in a place similar to where I was and be asking God why he left you, I remember feeling the same way, but fortunately for us, God knows more, and sees more than we do and at times needs to swoop in and save us from ourselves.*

God knew at that point in my life, I did not have the strength to leave him, so I believe with all of my heart that God had him leave me.

Painful though it was, I was forced to leave that night even though I had nowhere to go. Again, it was pouring rain that night. The rain outside suited how I felt inside. I took all my personal belongings (I really only had a few clothes), but my car was tiny, and it took up all the space in my car. I also had a huge stuffed tiger that Ned had won for me once at a carnival. I remember strapping my stuffed tiger into the passenger seat and buckling him in the seatbelt and pretending that he was God.

I talked to that stuffed tiger and believed that God was in the passenger seat with me so I wouldn't feel as alone as I felt and knew that I was. I had no idea where to go but I knew that I couldn't go very far because I had no money and I had to have enough gas in my car to get myself to work. I decided to park in the parking lot where I worked because I had no friends and believed at the time that I had no one to turn to. I cried myself to sleep as the rain bounced off my car and I eventually fell asleep in my Yellow VW Bug holding tight to my oversized stuffed tiger.

After a few days of living in my car I was at work and the manager called me into her office. I thought I had done something wrong. There was another employee in her office. Her name was Kristen, and she was still in high school and worked only part time. The manager asked me if I was okay. I lied and said yes even though my body language and my eyes said differently. She spoke in a very soft voice and told me that Kristen had noticed that I had all my belongings in my car and that my car was parked in the same exact spot for several days. The manager asked me if I had anyone to stay with and all I could do by this point was shake my head no. The employee that was in the room said to my manager, "She can spend the night at my house tonight."

I was more than embarrassed but I was also relieved that I didn't have to spend another night in my car. The kindness that this young high school girl showed me was overwhelming to me. She will never know how much hope she gave to me that day.

After work that night, I followed Kristen to her house, and I distinctly remember being in her bedroom and she asked me..." Can't you just go home?" I said, simply, "No." She asked if I had any other family and I told her that I did but that I was forbidden to ever contact any family or friends of my parents. She said, "Is there anyone that you know in your family that would stand up to your parents?" I thought about one of my mom's

younger sisters, my Aunt Hildi. She always talked back to my father, and I knew he did not like her, and I could tell that she did not like him. She was a very strong woman. I said, "My Aunt Hildi." She said, "Do you have her phone number?"
I honestly didn't know, but I had my address book that I had since I was a very little girl that someone had bought me for my birthday. It was a tall purple address book that had puppies playing on the front of it.
I opened it up and saw that I only had two addresses inside. One was my grandma and grandpa who I loved so very much and that brought tears to my eyes just seeing their name in my address book.
The other was my Aunt Hildi...

CHAPTER 7

Aunt Hildi

It was too late to call my Aunt Hildi, so I called her home number early the next morning before Kristen left for school and before I left to go to work.

I held my breath as the phone rang on the other end...

Finally, I heard my Aunt Hildi's strong and familiar voice, a voice that I knew by heart because I had heard her wonderful voice since I was born.

The minute I heard her voice, tears filled my eyes and started rolling down my cheeks. All I could say was, "Auntie Hildi," and I couldn't speak anymore. My aunt just said, "Faith, is that you?" I said, "yes." In between my sobbing.

Honestly, all I can remember is that she gave me her work number and told me to call her after I got off work and that she would meet me in the parking lot of where I worked and that I would follow her to her house.

I called her when I was ready to get off work and again it was pouring rain, but she found me in my little car in the parking lot of my work. I had my stuffed tiger in the passenger seat with his seat belt buckled. I held his stuffed paw as I followed my aunt in her car as it poured

rain. I was crying the whole way to my aunt's house. It felt like I was crying as hard as it was raining outside. I will never forget the song that was playing on the radio: "That's what friends are for," By Dion Warwick.
As I am writing this, I am playing that song in the background.
Honestly, that song still brings back so many feelings to me. I remember that all I had on my heart was God, and that is all I needed. He never forgot about me, and he played that song that dark, cold and rainy night to remind me that he had not forgotten about me.

Throughout the years I have heard that song and immediately upon hearing it, my eyes fill with tears, and I remember that God never forgot about me and that he was always going to be at my side, even if I needed to make believe he was present through my stuffed tiger....

I will never forget the first night that I spent at my Aunt Hildi and Uncle Stanley's house. I don't remember where my uncle was, but I remember I wandered into my aunt's room before she went to bed. My eyes were extremely swollen and red from all the crying I had been doing and I was still having trouble breathing right. I was doing everything I could to not cry anymore, and I blurted out, "I just want to be loved, I want someone to believe in me and to be proud of me." I started sobbing and put my hands over my face to protect me from the shame and humility that I felt. Suddenly, I felt my aunt grab one of my arms and I will never forget as long as I live what she said and did next...
she took my arm and put it around my back, and she

said these words: "<u>when there is no one to pat you on the back, then you pat yourself on the back and say, "Good Job Faith</u>!" and then she patted me on my back with my own hand.

She will never know how much that meant to me throughout my life, though I have tried to tell her many times. I have physically patted myself on the back so many times throughout my life that I can't even begin to count. That was one of the most profound moments of my life as well as a huge turning point for me.

I stayed at my Auntie Hildi and Uncle Stanley's house for about a month or so. I got there near Thanksgiving because I remember my grandma and grandpa came over to celebrate Thanksgiving along with other family members on my mother's side. I remember my grandma scolding me because I didn't call her and my grandpa. She told me that they were so worried about me. I would later find out that she and my grandfather were driving around at night in the city they thought I was living in to try to find me.
My grandma made me promise her that I would stay in contact with her and visit her and grandpa as much as I could.
I explained to both of my grandparents that my father had forbidden me to contact them or any friends or other members of the family. I told them that I didn't want them to get into trouble with my father. I will never forget the look on my grandmother's face. She had this look of disgust and anger all mixed into one and said, "I don't care what your father thinks, you are

my granddaughter, and I am always going to be on your side no matter what!"

Thinking about that now is bringing me to tears because the truth was, she and grandpa were always on my side. I still feel them with me.

I remember the week that I was ready to leave my Aunt Hildi's house, it was close to Christmas. I remember because I didn't have very much money and I wanted to do something nice for my aunt and uncle because they had let me stay with them while I got on my feet, so I bought a bunch of ingredients to bake them Christmas cookies.

I must begin telling you this part of my story by explaining that one of my greatest memories of my childhood was baking with my Aunt Hildi. Since I was a very little girl, my Aunt Hildi would have my two older brothers and I over her house before Christmas to stay with her for an entire weekend. We baked tons of Christmas cookies. In fact, My Aunt Hildi is the one who taught me to fall in love with baking and she was the one who taught me to bake. I remember one particular year, I had to be about six years old, and I was putting frosting on the cut-out cookies of The Peanut Gang. You know, Charlie Brown, Lucy, Linus and Snoopy. My aunt made me in charge of icing a Charlie Brown sugar cookie for one of my uncle's that I thought was particularly mean and let's just say he wasn't exactly my favorite at the time. Of course, my Aunt Hildi knew this, that was why she wanted me to frost him a cookie. What she didn't realize as I was frosting the cookie was that

I was using the green icing and icing Charlie Brown's nose. My aunt noticed what I was doing and asked me what the green frosting was on Charlie Brown's nose, and I said honestly, "Mocos." (Mocos was a word that in my family described boogers). Shortly after I made that cookie, who should come over but the uncle that the cookie was intended for. To my shock and surprise (not in a good way) my aunt tells my uncle, "Come look at the cookie Faith made for you." My face immediately turned red, and I froze. My uncle came to see the cookie and asked what the green frosting was meant for, and my aunt immediately answered: "Mocos!"

Before I could run away and hide, my uncle playfully picked me up and hit my head against the dishwasher. His actions proved to me that I made the perfect cookie for him!

My aunt later took us to the drive-in movies, in fact she took us to the first movie that I had ever gone to see at a movie theater.
"The Apple Dumpling Gang," with Don Knotts was the movie that we saw that night.
She drove us in her little dark green VW bug that she purchased the year I was born. It was one of the best days I ever had as a child, and one that I will never forget.

Again, some of the best times I ever had as a child were with my Aunt Hildi and the memories will always stay close to my heart.

On the second to last day that I was going to leave my

aunt's house to rent a room from my new boss's sister, my battery on my car died.

Both my aunt and my uncle were out of town on business, and it was going to be my first day at a new job as a receptionist for a law firm. When I realized my car wouldn't start and that I would probably get fired before I even started my new job, I did what I always did at this time in my life, I started to cry and to pray. Apparently, there was a lady across the street from my aunt's house watching me. She came over and knocked on my window. I rolled down the window and she told me that she noticed that I was having some problems with my car, so she took it upon herself to call the Automobile Club to come fix it for me for free. She told me that she told them that I was her daughter. I thanked her profusely. Within minutes someone came and got my battery to work. I never knew the name of that lady, but I knew where she lived so that night after work I went back to my aunt's house and finished baking all the cookies and I baked a little more. I had purchased two baskets and two cards, and I filled each of the baskets with freshly baked cookies with a card in each one. One I wrote to my aunt and uncle thanking them for everything and the other I wrote to the lady that saved me the day before. In her card, I wrote explaining how her kindness saved my new job. I wrote a bunch of meaningful words because I remember how it moved me when I wrote it to her, but I can't remember exactly what I wrote. I left it on her porch very early the next morning. My little car was packed full of all my belongings because I was leaving again to begin a new chapter in my life. I knew that I would take the skill set I learned while living in a positive environment with my aunt and uncle and I felt like I had hope for the very first time.

Things were looking up for me. As I told you before you can always find something good out of something bad. Ned had a workout partner named Dan and he had a wife and four kids. We used to spend time with them occasionally when we were together, and she saw a lot of my black eyes. She figured out that Ned was beating me and for some reason or another she cared about me. At one point she must have given me her phone number and told me if I ever needed anything to call her. Dan's wife was a manager at a law firm and somehow, I must have called her because she had offered me a receptionist job at the law firm that she worked at. This was the full-time job that I was starting the morning I left my aunt's house, and it was her sister that I was going to be renting a room from and moving into after my first day of my new job.

I was nervous and scared but as I said before I had a little bit of hope that I didn't have before.

Oftentimes in life we get overwhelmed by all the things that don't go the way we would like them to go in our lives. Often, they are huge and difficult things that we want to happen or don't want to happen but as I have said before we can only see what has happened in our past and oftentimes, we are too close to the situation to even see what is happening at the moment. This is the time when we need to trust in God's plan and ask him for signs to guide our way. Many times, in my life when I felt like God had left me, I later found that he was keeping me safe and trying to protect me from harm.

If you are in a place in your life where I have been in my past and you need guidance, please know there are many organizations that can help. You can also go to the website: **Voiceyourtruthministries.com**

CHAPTER 8

The Law Firm

For a while, I did very well at the law firm. The clients really liked me and would compliment me to the partners and the manager. I worked very hard and for 9 months or so, I was content at my job.

One of the partners at the firm I worked at was very nice to me because I would do a lot of extra work for him and never complain about it. We became friends, or so I thought. He was married and had 3 children that were toddlers and babies. His wife would often come into the office with the children, and she was always very nice.

I remember meeting the old receptionist before me. She was a few years older than I was, but she would come in and visit this attorney and go out to lunch with him. I never thought anything of it. However, she was always short with me and would make rude and embarrassing comments to me. I later realized that she had some sort of relationship with the attorney and was apparently jealous of me because she thought I did as well.

The law firm was expanding and had been building new offices on the entire floor that we were on.

One Friday at the end of my workday there were a few attorneys and partners still hanging out talking. As I was just about to leave the office for the weekend the partner that was my friend asked me if I had seen the new receptionist area where they were going to be moving me to when all the new offices were complete. I said, "No, not yet." He said he would show me on the way out. I was excited to see it. I remember walking out the office doors and following him towards all these tarps covering the future offices. My new desk was made of marble. I went closer to take a better look at the desk and was in awe of how fancy it was. I was amazed that I would be sitting at such a regal desk. When I turned around to tell my friend how excited I was, he had his pants down to his ankles and his penis was hanging out and he told me to give him oral sex. I was in shock, and I panicked. I ran right past him and went down the elevator as fast as it would go. I was both disgusted and devastated that he would do that to me. I remember thinking, "What is wrong with me?" "Why do men keep doing this to me?" I thought I was finally free from having this kind of thing happen to me, but I was wrong. The partner was about 35 or 36 years old, and I was barely 19 years old.

To this day, I do not understand why this attorney took it upon himself to expose himself to me and demand me to do such disgusting things to him.

I remember doing a lot of crying that weekend.

On Monday, as soon as I walked in the door the office manager that hired me, called me into her office and asked me to close the door. I sat down and she proceeded to fire me.

She said she got some very bad complaints from one of the partners and that she had no choice but to let me go. I could tell that she didn't want to fire me and that she felt bad. She told me that there were so many other things that I could do. I remember her telling me that I should try to be a model because I was so beautiful. All I could do was cry. Rejected again.

I was so used to keeping secrets and was brainwashed for so long that when things like this happened to me, I believed somehow, I was to blame for them. It never even occurred to me to tell her what had happened on that Friday after work.

To be honest, at the time this occurred I didn't really understand fully that he was to blame. *I believe that stemmed from the sexual abuse that I endured from my father.*

Little did I know at the time, but I could have sued that law firm and I could have done a lot of damage to that partner and the whole firm for that matter.

Thinking back, I remember another situation at that firm. The firm was having an open house for the clients, and it was a party atmosphere. I was working and passing out appetizers to all the clients and attorney's when a different and newer partner made some sexual comments to me. I just ignored him and walked away. He made that comment in front of one of the other attorneys in the firm and apparently it got back to the office manager and the two main partners. They wrote a letter to me apologizing to me and blaming the poor conduct on the alcohol that the partner was drinking. I was so young, so scared and so embarrassed. I thought that I must be doing something bad for so many men to be acting that way towards me. I am sure that it stemmed from my own father telling me how bad I was and forcing me to go to confession all the time.

Although what I went through was painful, I realize that I would have never met my friend Jack and his family if I hadn't worked there.

I met Jack at the law firm. He was in his first years of college and worked part time for the firm making copies, running errands and any odd jobs they needed. He was nice to me and although I was very shy, we became friends. He introduced me to his cousin Mia and eventually they both became my best friends. They were Dutch Indonesian, and I eventually met all their family. I spent a lot of time at both of their homes. They both lived at home with their parents. Their families became my families, and I will always be forever grateful for that time and for the love and kindness that they shared with me.

My relationship with Mia, Jack and their family eventually helped me with my codependency that I had with Ned. I would go back to Ned time and time again allowing him to use me for his personal needs. I was so young and so naive that I just kept following my heart. Of course, not using the brain God gave me got me into a lot of trouble and a lot of unneeded pain. Ned always seemed to keep me around on the back burner but eventually I got strong enough to tell him to stop calling me and coming to my work. Mia, Jack, and their family were good influences on me and knew that Ned was not good for me, so they helped me find the strength inside myself that I needed to move on. Now I realize that at the time I believed myself to be so in love with him but in reality, I was codependent on him, and I was in an abusive relationship that was extremely unhealthy for me. Although I dated a lot of other guys, I never fully got over him until later in life.

When I was about 24 years old, I had been working at a small business that I loved for a few years already when I received a call at work from Ned. When I heard his voice, fear swept through me for a moment. My first thought was, "How did he find me?" As quickly as the fear came, it left me, and I was filled with anger. How dare he contact me. My voice was harsh and to the point, "How did you get my number?" He said he ran into Jane and that she gave him my number. I told him not to ever call me again and then I hung up the phone. I made a mental note to never speak to Jane again. However, he immediately called me back and I answered the call because it was a work phone, and it could have been clients of our office calling. It was him. He immediately said to please not to hang up. He wanted to apologize for how he treated me when we were together. For some reason I let him speak and I didn't hang up.

He proceeded to tell me that he was on steroids (which I knew) when we were together and that one of the common side effects from taking steroids was extreme anger. He apologized for beating me and for how horribly he treated me. Then he asked me for something I never thought he would ask for, forgiveness. When he said the words, the huge wall of anger that embodied me dissolved and at that moment, I forgave him. For the first time since we had broken up, I had the healing that I longed for. God took all the hurt and pain and cast it far away from me. That day I had closure to a toxic, abusive, and unhealthy relationship. I realize now that I am older that the forgiveness wasn't really for him, it was for me. I didn't have to carry all the pain and anger around with me anymore, I could let it go so that God could heal me and make room for more love in my heart.

If you are in an abusive relationship, I want you to know that I understand firsthand what you are going through. You are not alone. There is help there for you and I want to remind you that God has never left you nor will he ever leave or forsake you. We are loved far better by our creator than anyone in this world could ever love us.

CHAPTER 9
Tanta Nora

I was especially close to Mia's mom; Tanta Nora (Auntie Nora). She was strong and tough, yet still funny, kind and loving.

Tanta Nora used to make soup and always had white rice to put in your bowl and pour the soup on top of so the rice wouldn't get mushy. I loved it. She would make fried egg rolls with cabbage and meat inside and peanut sauce for dipping. That was my favorite! I haven't had it in years.

I loved Tanta Nora very much; she was the closest thing to a mom that I had in my life at the time. Just thinking about her now brings tears to my eyes. I found out a few years ago that Tanta Nora died a while back. I never realized while I was around her how much she meant to me, so I never had the chance to share with her how I felt about her. She never knew that I had a huge hole in my heart where a mother's love was supposed to be. Nor did I tell her that for a time she helped fill a bit of my heart with those egg rolls, peanut sauce and her vegetable soup with the rice cooker filled with rice. I never told her how hungry I always was for lack of money to buy food. I never told her that her big bear hug she gave me filled my eyes with tears because it was the only form of affection I ever received during those times. *I was so afraid of how my father would treat my grandparents that I failed them again and stayed away to protect all of them. I* never told her how safe I felt spending the night at her house. "Tanta Nora, wherever you are, thank you from the 19-year-old Faith and from the 56-year-old woman that I now am."

During this time in my life, I started dating a lot to get over Ned. I did not sleep with all the men that I dated but I did have sex with some.

I am only mentioning this for those of you that are feeling badly about the choices you have made in your life, you are not alone, we all make bad choices at different times in our lives. The important thing is that we learn from our mistakes and grow from them.

The only time I ate was when I went on a date or I ate at Tanta Nora's house, I had very little money at this time. I could basically pay my rent and either eat or put gas in my car. Most of the time I chose to put gas in my car so that I could get to work. I never had a credit card until after I was married, and I was 26 years old.
One rainy night when I got home from work and parked my car on the street, I was trying to decide whether to get something to eat the next morning or to use my last $5.00 to put gas in my car, when I saw a homeless man across the street laying on the sidewalk in the rain. I took my $5.00 and gave it to the homeless man.

The next morning, I went out to my car that was parked all by itself with no other cars on the street and I was about to get into my car when I looked down on the ground next to my car and found a $50 dollar bill. I believe that it was God sending me money because I had given my last $5.00 to help someone else that was worse off than I was. I believe that God helps us when we need it and when we are helping others especially at times when it isn't easy for us.

I know that God blessed me 10-fold that day. I won't ever forget that lesson that I learned from doing the right thing.

At that time in my life, I couldn't even afford to buy tampons or toilet paper. I would go to public restrooms and take rolls of toilet paper that I would use instead of using pads or tampons because I couldn't afford them.

I remember being so hungry one night when I came home from work and came home to my roommate making popcorn and it smelled so delicious. I was so hungry from not eating for a few days that I would come home and cry myself to sleep.

Of course, I never told my friends, my roommate or Tanta Nora anything about those things.

The walls that I created to protect myself ended up hurting me in many ways. I kept everything to myself about me, my life, and my family situation. I am sure that if my roommate or my friends knew about what I was going through, they would have helped me. But I had too much pride and I didn't want anyone to know anything about me. I identify with turtles because I call it turtling up when I go into my shell and hide. Not telling anyone anything about myself and hiding who I am is me turtling up.

For most of my life I tried to protect myself and didn't allow people to get too close to me. I would be there for them, but I didn't allow anyone to be there for me. That was another example of me hiding in my shell or "Turtling Up."

It has taken me many years and a lot of work to open up and share who I really am with people. I know that at times I will forever be the turtle, but I realize now that a turtle comes out of its shell sometimes. Fortunately, the desire to help others and to lead them to God pushes me out of my shell.

Whenever I make chicken soup, I always make a side of sticky rice in my rice cooker for those I love. I am honoring the beautiful lady that treated me like she was my mom and showing those I love the way I was taught by such a humble and beautiful human being. Chicken soup and sticky rice will always bring a sense of warmth and love to my heart because it will remind me of a time when it brought me joy when I needed it most.

I realize now that although I didn't have my own mom in my life, God always put wonderful women in my life when I needed them most. I am forever thankful and grateful to God for that.

CHAPTER 10
Mexico

I was 20 years old, I just got fired from a job I had worked at for a year that I really should have never been hired for in the first place. I was going out dancing with my friends every night of the week and hardly sleeping at all because often by the time I got home from going out it was time to get up and get ready for work. I was wild and just wanted to have fun. I was like a caged animal for much of my life, so I just wanted to be free and feel like I was alive. Obviously, that came with a price, losing my job was the price I paid for my freedom and my carefree attitude.

Of course, I quickly realized that I could not continue to live my life the way I was living it because I wasn't going anywhere but in the wrong direction. I don't really remember how or why I ended up at my dad's place of business but all I remember was sitting in his office asking him if he could help me pay for college and that I would pay him back because I knew I wasn't going anywhere with my life and I needed to learn some skills.

Why I ever went to him in the first place is beyond me because when I was 17 years old he made my mom go down

*to my high school and take me out of school permanently.
I want to also reiterate that at this age in my life, I did not
understand that my father was a bad and unsafe person to
be around. I had been brainwashed that I was the bad and
evil one and I believed that for most of my life.*

My father said he would make a deal with me, and he
would pay for a full 4 years of college if I did something
for him. He wanted me to go live in Mexico as a
volunteer for a year. I immediately said, no. Then he
said something he knew would get to me. He said,
"They need you in Mexico, you would be able to help so
many people."

All I ever wanted was to be needed and to help people.
The phrase: Hook, line and sinker comes to mind.
I did end up going to live in Mexico. I weighed 115 pounds
before I left (and was still underweight) and when I
returned, I weighed only 85 pounds. I was gone for a
total of six months. I didn't realize it at the time, but my
father was trying to get rid of me, I believe to this day it
was in more ways than one.
He wanted me away from him, away from the area he
lived in and away from anyone that he knew.

I was so naive. I had no idea what he was planning. I
was just desperate and didn't know where else to turn
so I made the mistake of trusting him. A very bad thing
for me to do with someone like him, but again I was
naive and did not realize at this point in my life (I was 20
years old) that what my father did to me throughout my
childhood was not my fault.

My father went to Catholic school when he was young and somehow when he got older, he had reconnected with a nun that used to be his teacher. She lived in Mexico and started and ran a nursing school for the young people that lived there.

He used to donate money to her all the time. Most of the time she lived in Mexico but came to the United States every six months to keep her citizenship in good standing.

I have known this nun since I was a little girl. She seemed like she was nice back then, but when I moved to Mexico to help her with the school, I found out the hard way that I was very wrong.

She was extremely fake and nice to anyone that had money so that they would give her money for the school and for herself. If you didn't have any money, she had no use for you. She was a very mean, conceited, and a very selfish person. Not my definition of anyone supposed to be close to God.

Her two great nephews; Samuel and Luca came to Mexico for a two-week vacation and traveled with us to Mexico (They were both freshmen in high school).

I brought my life savings with me so that I could write to my family (my mom and my grandparents) and to my friends. I also wanted to make sure that I would always have food.

The first day we were in Mexico we went to the bank and Sister Juanita made me deposit most of my money into her bank account except for enough for me to purchase some stamps.

I spent the first two weeks spending time with the boys and Sister Juanita and for the most part everything was ok, except for me getting monazuma's revenge after about a week of being there. The first week we got there we went on long drives to some surrounding cities because Sister Juanita wanted her great nephews to have a good time.

She encouraged me to take out money from the bank account that she had opened for me so that we could do some sightseeing and I could pay for all the food for everywhere we went (but I could only get into the account if she was with me).

The boys were about 14 and 15 years old and the three of us got very close. We used to listen to Luca's music that he brought with him to Mexico. It was, "The Cure." To this day when I hear a song from, "The Cure," I still think of Luca. I could tell that Luca had a very sad 14 years and did not have a good home life. He opened up to me and told me about his pain, all I could do at that time was listen. I wasn't brave enough to share anything about me or my life and didn't understand any of what I had lived through most of my life to share anything with him about my life that could help him. I didn't even know how to help myself at that point in my life.

When the two weeks were almost over both boys could already tell how mean Sister Juanita was, especially to me. The boys were worried about leaving me there in Mexico because we all could tell that everything was going to get much worse for me once the boys left.

It was extremely difficult for me and the boys to say goodbye but when the day came, we did what we had

to do and said our sad goodbyes. Luca gave me his
tape cassette player and all his, "The Cure," tapes. That
was the last time I ever spoke to or saw the boys. Luca
wrote me a couple of letters but eventually we lost touch
because I wasn't allowed to have any of the money to
buy stamps so I couldn't write him back. I couldn't even
write to my mom or my grandparents.

Sister Juanita would not allow me to take any more
money out of the bank. I needed money for stamps and
for food even though she was supposed to be feeding
me three meals a day. I lived off old coffee and week-old
bread rolls. I was literally starving.

Before I left the states to go to Mexico with Sister Juanita,
she had told me that some of the village girls would ask
me to go to their homes to share a meal with them and
that it would be good for me to experience the different
cultures and see how each lived.

The first week we were there she allowed me to go with
a girl that was a few years older than I was that worked
in the school office and lived nearby. Her name was
Alicia. I was invited to her home for lunch. For the life
of me, I cannot remember what we ate but I am sure
it was good.

A few weeks after the boys left the fall school year was
starting so some of the girls that lived in far away villages
came and lived in the big house where I lived. I shared
a very tiny room with Sister Juanita's adopted daughter
Lupita who was about 10 years old. She was filthy and
she was a thief. For the life of me, I don't understand
why Sister Juanita didn't have Lupita live in the private
apartment house above the house we lived in with

her. She was more like a little slave than an adopted daughter. I felt very sorry for her, but I also felt sorry for myself because she stole so many of my personal things and she always had a lot of lice in her hair. I was paranoid that I was going to get it because I lived in such tight living quarters with her.

There was only one restroom for about 15 girls to share (During the week they lived in the same building where I lived). The bathroom had two toilets sitting side by side and one shower. We did not have any hot water, so it was the coldest water I had ever felt in my life. I learned how to take really quick showers because not only was the water freezing, but there was a line outside the bathroom door with girls waiting to use the toilet and the shower. As soon as one person was either done showering or going to the bathroom another person would go inside and take their turn. At first it was awful and humiliating because there was absolutely no privacy (Especially since I was so shy). As time went by, some of the best conversations I had were when two of us were sitting side by side going to the bathroom.

I was asked by many of the girls that were in the nursing school to go home with them on the weekends. However, Sister Juanita would not allow me to ever go. I would be left alone the entire weekend. I hated Fridays. I was so lonely and so homesick. The other girl that moved into our tiny room shared the bunk bed with Lupita (The room had only one single bed and a bunk bed right next to it and they were almost touching). Nothing else fit in the room. The girl's name was Maria Elena.

She also graduated from the nursing school and worked
at the school. At first, she was mean to me. We couldn't
communicate at first, well actually no one spoke English
and I did not speak Spanish.

When the two of us were at the school working is when
and where I originally met Maria Elena. It was obvious
to me that she did not like me. Once she moved into my
room and was living in such tight quarters with me, we
became best friends.

She taught me Spanish, and I taught her English. We
studied every day and eventually I started dreaming in
Spanish because I never spoke or heard English. I forgot
to mention that we had no heat or air conditioning in
the house we lived in. I got to Mexico in June and left a
few days before Christmas, so I experienced the worst
of the heat and the worst of the cold. I later found out
that sister Juanita had heat and air conditioning along
with a regular kitchen with a lot of food in the fridge
and pantry.

She lived like a queen as she starved me.

Maria Elena made about $2.00 a week and when she got
paid, I would go to the Mercado (store) after work with
her and she would buy cheese and tortillas. It is because
of Marie Elena that I didn't starve to death. She shared
her food with me all week. She would go home on Friday,
and we would both cry because she knew she was
leaving me all alone and I wouldn't eat, and I would be
so sad and so lonely. On Sunday's her mom would make
me this sweet corn stuff wrapped in a banana leaf. Maria
Elena and her family were very poor. She lived in a little
village and in a little hut. They didn't even have a stove,

they had to cook on a little fire they made in the middle of the room. Maria Elena was a Telaskin Indian. She was one of the most generous people I will ever know. It was especially humbling to come from the United States where I took a lot for granted to a very poor country where a poor Mexican Indian girl gave me generously half of what she had.

For the first time in my life, I found out what the true meaning of the word "friend" really meant.

About the second week after I arrived in Mexico, I got an infection in both of my eyes. I later found out that it was a bacterial infection. Both of my eyes were filled with a green sticky goo that would seal my eyes closed every night. In the morning it would take me about 10 minutes of soaking each of my eyes with water to open them. I told Sister Juanita about it and asked her if there was anything she could do to help me, but she said no and did absolutely nothing to help me.

As soon as I came back to the states my mother saw my eyes and immediately took me to the doctors. The doctor said that if I would have gone one more day without the drops, he prescribed me I would have gone blind in both of my eyes.

Before I left the states to go to Mexico, my mom said she would call me while I was in Mexico. I never received a phone call from her but after about a month of being there, one of the girls that lived in the same place I lived in told me that my mom called, and Sister Juanita told her I wasn't there and that I had gone home with one of the girls. I soon found out that she was playing interference with all the calls my mother made to me. I realize now that sister Juanita did not want me to tell my mom about my living conditions and lack of food. We had to go back to the states for Christmas so that Sister Juanita could keep her citizenship.

Maria Elena was sure I wouldn't come back. I promised her I would come back, and I wanted to come back to Mexico. I was so sure that I was coming back to Mexico that I left all my photos and all my belongings. My camera, everything I owned that I had taken to Mexico.

When my mother saw me at the airport, she looked shocked and worried. As soon as we got a minute alone, she told me that she wasn't letting me go back and was disgusted with Sister Juanita.
My mom could not believe that Sister Juanita did absolutely nothing to help my eyes when she ran a nursing school, and it would have been extremely easy for her to give me some drops for my eyes. When she saw how skinny I was, she realized how poorly Sister Juanita cared for me. She asked me why I didn't write to her or call. When I told her about the money and that sister Juanita wouldn't let me have my money, she was furious. The next day she took me to the doctors and when the doctors told us that I could have gone blind, she got into a big fight with my father and told him that there was no way in hell that she was going to let me go back.
Believe it or not, I begged to go back to Mexico because I had made a promise to my friend, Maria Elena. As you have probably already guessed, my father never

paid one penny for me to go to college. I never went to college.

He had me start working at his business that he owned, underpaying me, and treating me like a mistreated dog. One day he was in a particularly bad mood and yanked my purse out of my hands and threw everything out on the ground.

For the life of me, I cannot remember what he said I did. Back then I had barely saved enough money to buy a small mirror, and a lipstick and he broke both, along with my purse.

He shoved me to the ground and started kicking me. It was so humiliating because there was a guy that was working in the office and saw the whole thing. I was already 21 years old, and I finally had enough. I left crying that day and never went back.

I wouldn't change my experience in Mexico for anything. I learned many valuable lessons.

I learned how someone so poor could be so rich because of how generous they were. I learned to share whatever I have with those in need because I am so grateful for having so much and I know what it is like firsthand to not have enough to eat.

When I had nothing to eat, someone that had almost nothing shared what she had with me.

I learned that not speaking the same language as someone else does not prevent love and friendship.

When I came home from living in Mexico, I learned to slow down and to take time to talk to people and to listen.

Not just with family and friends but at the grocery store, at the bank, at fast food restaurants, wherever I went.

I noticed a lot more and paid attention to the details that most people didn't notice.

I learned not to take things or people for granted.

I appreciated spending time talking and listening to people.

I grew a lot, and I learned the true meaning of the word friendship. I learned how rich a person could be even though they didn't have any money or material things (Thank you Maria Elena, wherever you are).

I came home humbled, more gracious, and truly thankful for all the blessings that I had in my life.

I learned to appreciate all the things that I had taken for granted, like taking a shower with hot water!

CHAPTER 11

Steve

I was living with my former manager from the Law Firm, the one that fired me two years before, she was divorced and a single mother of four children. I met Steve after an entire weekend of crying and hiding in the room I was renting in a friend's house.

My life was a mess as usual. I was 21 years old, and I was dating many men, none of which I loved and none of which loved me. I was more lonely than usual and missed having a family of my own. After crying for almost three days straight I decided to go to the Catholic church near my house. I hadn't been to church in at least three or four years, and I knew that the possibilities of finding the answers to the questions that I asked could quite possibly be found there. I arrived in the empty church about 4:00 in the afternoon and sat in an empty pew in an empty church.

I got down on my knees and prayed as hard and as deeply as only one other time in my life, when I was a small child.

I remember my prayer; I remember every word as if just spoken today. I first told God how lonely I was and how I missed my family. I told him how empty I was and how

I didn't want to be alone anymore. I begged, I pleaded, I bargained and all the while I cried. I told God I was ready to let go of all the men I was dating and promised not to see any of them anymore if he would just introduce me to the man that he wanted me to marry. I asked God to please make him perfectly clear to me so that I would know that God had sent him to me. I told God repeatedly that I needed him to give me huge signs so that I would recognize whomever he sent as the one that he had chosen for me. Suddenly, through my deep prayer and buckets of tears that poured out both from my eyes and my nose, I realized that mass was starting and that I needed to get out of there quickly before anyone saw me in the state, I was in. To my dismay it was too late. Just as I was going to leave the pew, a guy came and sat down on the end next to me. I started to turn in the other direction but a whole family came in on the other side of me which pushed me closer to the guy on the end of the pew. I felt extremely uncomfortable but the only thing I could do was sit through mass and avoid eye contact with anyone. So, that is exactly what I did. I remember he had big hands; I remember looking around the church when we stood up and wondering if the people around me thought that the guy next to me was with me. I remember the loneliness leaving me as this guy held my hand during the Lord's Prayer. I remember how safe I felt holding those big hands and how safe I had felt for the thirteen years that followed. The man that sat next to me was Steve. He didn't ask me out that day, but I knew in my heart, although I didn't even know what he looked like, that he was the one God had sent to me. All I remembered as I left the church that day is that he had redish hair and big hands (Like my grandfather).

The next week I was out of town with some friends. I thought about that guy the entire week. The following week I went back to church, but I went for the 5:00pm mass. I sat in the same seat as two weeks prior and as soon as I sat down Steve sat down next to me. I later found out that he was at the river the same weekend I was out of town and that he was waiting to see if I would come back to church. Still, he didn't ask me out. He did not speak to me except for wishing me peace when it was time for us to say peace be with you to everyone. Steve sat next to me every single Sunday after that day and at one point spoke to me after mass, but never asked me out until Sunday, the 29th day of October in 1988. We were leaving church and by this point it had already been 3 months of not dating and waiting for Steve to ask me out. I was ready to give up on him and started doubting if he was the one God meant for me. We were exiting church and Steve asked me, "Are you coming to the 5:00pm mass next Sunday?" I was surprised by his question and answered, "I guess so, why?" He said, "If you come to mass next week maybe we can grab a bite to eat." I said, "Okay." I said goodbye. I wasn't quite sure if he was asking me out just as a friend or not because he was so nonchalant. When I realized he had finally asked me out, I rounded the corner, I jumped in the air and raised one arm up and said, "YES!" I knew at that very moment that God had sent Steve to me and that he was the one that God wanted me to marry. The next week I got to church and there was no sign of Steve. At that moment I thought that I was wrong and that he had not asked me out on a date, but he was just being friendly. Halfway through mass I had to concentrate on not letting my tears fall down my cheeks and at that exact moment, Steve came and sat down next to me. *It just goes to show that when you have finally given up, God hasn't given up on you or your situation and he always comes through.* He was apologizing for being late, I remember shushing him because he was talking too loudly. But inside, I couldn't help feeling relieved. He said he was late because it was his niece's birthday. As we were leaving church, he turned to me and asked if I wanted to get something to eat. I said, "That sounds great." He asked where I wanted to go and I said, "anywhere is fine." He suggested that we go to a restaurant nearby and I said, "sure." I had never been to the restaurant that we went to before but that night it became one of my favorite restaurants. The minute we walked through the door, I remember two small girls ran up to me and hugged me. They were little girls that lived in the neighborhood I lived in. That night as we sat down to eat dinner, Steve told me that he was married and that he was in the middle of going through a divorce. For a split second I told myself; "don't like him," because I always dreamed of marrying someone that had never been married before. I wanted a fairytale romance and marriage. But by my next thought, it was too late because I was already developing feelings for him.

Our dating and marriage were a far cry from a fairytale

story, but then we did have a beautiful Princess named Sierra and a handsome Prince named Declan.

I had never told Steve about all the abuse I endured during my childhood prior to our marriage and that was not fair to him. I made a lot of poor choices that hurt our marriage and Steve. I am truly sorry for them. I didn't even know who I was when I married Steve at the age of 25 because all I was ever taught about myself were lies from the two people that were supposed to love me and protect me. I tried for so long to suppress all of what happened to me, but I always knew the truth and eventually the truth always comes out.

Steve and I were separated for ten months in the year 2000. During that time, I finally told my therapist what had happened to me so many years before. I was going to my weekly appointments and then I started going to a two-hour group therapy. The truth of my past was too much for my mind, my heart, and my body to bear. I ended up getting so sick I started going in and out of the hospital every week. I could only eat when I had my kids, and I would still get very ill. I was happiest when I had my kids so my therapist told me to try to eat as much as I could when I was with them. I remember seeing one of the guys that worked with Steve one morning at the doughnut shop by my house. Apparently, the guy told Steve that he saw me and was concerned by how sick I looked from all the weight I had lost. Bringing all the abuse and pain up from the most hidden locked vault in my mind was killing me. I remember one Saturday talking on the phone to my

Uncle Stanley (He and my Aunt Hildi were the only ones besides my therapist that knew about the abuse I had endured throughout my childhood). My uncle told me that I had to tell Steve about everything because if I didn't, I was going to die. He proceeded to tell me that the only way I would survive is if I went back to live with Steve. He told me that he didn't care if I had to beg him to take me back, but if I didn't tell Steve then he would tell him.

I ended up telling Steve everything and we got back together for a year and a half.

I got healthy being able to spend time with my kids everyday. I continued my therapy and worked through a lot of pain. I honestly don't know if Steve ever knew that he saved my life back then or what a huge difference that he made in my life. Steve was the first one to provide me with the security and safety that I had longed for my whole life.

I will always be forever grateful for everything Steve did for me and most of all for the two beautiful children that he blessed me with.

On December 10th, 2002, our divorce was final. Steve came over to my house and handed me his copy of the final divorce decree and said, "we are divorced now." I remember that both of us had tears in our eyes and he hugged me.

When we had finally decided to divorce, I knew that it was the right decision for both of us. However, I struggled with the idea of divorcing Steve because I felt that God had brought him to me and answered my prayer when we met, especially since we met in church. One day before the divorce was final, I talked to him about my hesitation. I will never forget what he told me...

"You asked God to introduce you to the man he wanted you to marry, not who he wanted you to spend the rest of your life with."

Steve was right in telling me that and I learned how important it is to pray for discernment in our decisions in our lives. I believe that sometimes situations in our lives change and at those crossroads we need to ask God for guidance. We need to ask for signs for direction and we need to look for the signs. God put's many signs in front of us daily, the problem is we get so busy in our lives that we don't remember to look for them and even when the signs are right in front of us, we are so preoccupied that we fail to see them.

CHAPTER 12
grandpa

My grandpa was one of the two people in this world that I knew that truly loved me. He showed me love ever since I could remember. He was always proud to pick me up when I was a little girl and put me up on the counter at the bank to show me off to all the tellers.

My grandfather always had a huge smile on his face with love and kindness in his eyes. He loved to tease me, and he teased me well. I was my grandpa's princess. *Just writing that last line filled my eyes with tears and flooded my heart with pain because he is no longer here to call me his princess or to tell grandma to call "our" princess to check on me.* He was always protective of me and showed his love for me well. When I would take him to dialysis, we would hold hands all the way there and all the way home. I knew I was on borrowed time with grandpa for a very long time. I always told him how much I loved him, and I always picked his brain about life because he had lived so long and so well. About two months before he died, my grandma, my two small children and I were driving grandpa home from dialysis. I asked grandpa if he had ever seen the movie, "City of Angels." He said no. I explained the very beginning of the movie as I am going to do now. I told him in the first scene there was a child that was very sick in her bed and her mother was praying for God not to take her child. Well, sadly the child dies, and the Angel of Death played by, Nicholas Cage asks the child as they are walking down a hall, "What was your favorite thing in life?" The little girl answered quickly, "Pajamas." That first part in the movie really impacted my life so much that I had to ask my grandparents what their favorite things were. So, as I was holding grandpa's hand, I asked him what his favorite thing was, his answer was simply, "grandma." I said, "Oh no, you can't pick a person, you have to name a thing. Grandpa had a big smile on his face and said, "grandma" a few more times and finally when my persistence paid off, he said, "Love, peace, faith and kindness." Well, after that, I couldn't argue with him. That was the kind of man that he was, he cared about people, and he cared about feelings. There was no one person in this world that grandpa teased more than my poor grandma. My grandma had a name for my grandpa. She called him her Big Bug. Grandpa would take his big hand and put it on top of grandma's head and say in a deep voice: "Bug, Bug, Bug."

My grandparents had 61 years of marriage and love. It is painful to hear my grandmother's voice or see the sadness that lingers in her eyes.

On a personal note, it has been a very difficult time for me because this loss was so great. Not only did I love my wonderful grandfather, but I lost my father figure and role model and one of my core sources of love. I did not have a consistency of love that I could see daily, but the

way grandma and grandpa loved me was the core love I
received as a child and throughout my life.
My grandmother refused to listen to music for a few
years after grandpa died because she loved music so
much and it brought her so much joy. She didn't want
to have any joy because she was heartbroken without
my grandpa, and I think maybe she felt guilty if she
listened to music.

Eventually one Christmas I took a bunch of Christmas
rubber stamps; card stock and accessories and I
designed Christmas cards for my grandma and I to
make for her Chrstmas cards to send out. It was the first
time that she listened to music since my grandpa had
passed away. It was Christmas music. This started a new
tradition for my grandmother and me. Every year we
would make her Christmas cards to send out to family
and friends.

My grandfather was the most patient human being I
have ever known, he was also the most generous.
My grandmother told me that more than once when
her and my grandpa had gone out to dinner with
family or friends, he would be missing for a long period
of time and then she would see him at another table
with the homeless people that she had previously seen
sitting outside the restaurant. He had brought them
into the restaurant to feed and to eat dinner with them.
I wish there were more people like my grandfather
and grandma in the world. This world would be such a
better place.

When I found out my grandpa had a stroke, I had just

started my new job as a Mortgage Consultant, and I had just recently gotten a divorce.

I quickly went straight to the hospital. My grandfather was in a coma. I called my new boss and told him that I was sorry but that he would have to fire me because I had to be with my grandma and be at the hospital with my grandpa until he either got better or he died. He was a good boss because he told me to take the time I needed, and he kept paying me a salary.

I was always at the hospital when I didn't have my children. On the Thursday that they "pulled the plug" I was alone in the hospital room with my grandma and my grandpa because my aunts and uncle were making funeral arrangements. The nurse came in as grandma and grandpa and I were all holding hands. I was praying out loud and crying. I remember having a stretch bracelet on my wrist on the hand that I was holding my grandma and my grandpa's hand. My grandfather couldn't open his eyes and he couldn't speak. But what he did do was try to tease me one last time before he died. He pushed my grandma's hand away and I don't know how but he got my bracelet off my wrist with one hand and put it on his own wrist. I will never know how he did it, but I do know why. He knew that I was hurting and devastated that he was going to die, and he was trying to make me laugh.

I remember something significant before the nurse came in to turn off all the machines...

My grandma took my hand, and she told me something that caught me off guard. She told me that she knew that there was something that I wasn't telling her and that it was okay if I didn't want to tell her but that she knew whatever it was that I wasn't telling her was getting in the way of being even closer than we already were. She told me that she knew that I would tell her when I was ready. She squeezed my hand and kissed me on the cheek.

I would later end up telling her about that secret that I was keeping from her because of this moment in the hospital.

It was a few months later, a time that was not planned but that just happened.

I used to take grandma and grandpa to eat at a place called Spike's to get chicken bowls with rice and we would add avocado on top. On this day, my kids were in school. My grandpa had passed away a few months before, so grandma and I were in the car alone. The last time my grandma saw my mom it was at my grandfather's funeral. My mom never saw my grandma again after the funeral, and my grandma was very upset about it. I saw my grandma at least 2 to 3 times a week and she would talk about not understanding why my mom was being so mean to her and had stopped calling or taking her calls.

I knew why she was not taking my grandma's calls and distancing herself. It was because of me because of how close I was to my grandma. My heart was getting too heavy just sitting there seeing how hurt my grandma was, thinking that she had done something wrong to offend my mom. My grandma did not deserve to get treated this way by anyone, especially because of me.

As we turned into Spike's parking lot, my grandma was being very sad and upset about my mom. As I said before, I never planned on telling my grandma, I hadn't wanted her to know the truth about what my father had done to me during my childhood. I couldn't let her continue to think that she had done something wrong with my mom. I had to free her of any guilt or bad feelings about my mom. I had to tell her the truth about why my mom had ended the relationship with her and how I am sure it was all Damian's doing. So, I took a deep breath and parked my car and looked directly into the face of my grandma and I told her...

"Remember what you said to me when we were alone in the hospital room with grandpa when they pulled the plug?" She looked at me not really understanding where this was going but I continued anyway and told her about my father.

I never saw my grandma cry so much in my entire life. I felt awful. She did however thank me for telling her the truth and for trusting her with the information that I told her.
She did in fact understand at that moment why my mom had distanced herself from her and realized that she would never again have any kind of relationship with my mom. My grandma was angry with my mom for her decision to choose her husband over her daughter, over her mother and over what was right and just.
I am sad that my grandma had to know the very sad truth about me, but I was happy that she finally understood me completely and why I did the things I

did and acted the way I acted. My grandma had thought that I was lost when I turned 18 and left home, now she knows that I left for my own survival. The truth is that I was lost but in a different way then she initially thought. There has never been a love in my life as strong as the love of my grandma. She wasn't my biological blood grandma, but she was my heart grandma. There are people in life that we were born into, biological mother's, father's, brother's, sister's, grandma's, grandpa's, nieces, nephews, etc. However, there are mother's, father's, brother's, sister's, grandma's, grandpa's, nieces, and nephews etc. that God brings into our lives to fill our empty holes in our hearts with the love and appreciation that was meant to be there from the beginning. When the people in our lives that were meant to protect and love us fail, God always comes through.

He has always come through for me.

A real family are the people in your life that are there when you need them the most, the people that see you, know you, hear you and love you anyway.

I am blessed to have a whole family that God chose for me personally. I don't cry over the people in my life that were supposed to be a part of my biological family but chose not to be or that I believed were not safe enough or healthy enough to be around my children or me.

It took me a very long time to "let go" of the huge desire to have my mom in my life and in the lives of my children. One thing that stands out in my mind that helped me (besides lots of praying and one on one time with God) was the Disney movie for children, "Finding Nemo."

I remember the first time I watched it and when I came to one part in the movie where Nemo was in the whale and Dory said, "Just Let Go." For some reason, I started sobbing and at that very moment, I knew that God was telling me through a cartoon movie to let go of obsessing over wanting and needing my mom so desperately.

Little by little, day by day, I did start letting go of the need to have her present in my life and in the lives of my children. It didn't happen overnight, but I did learn to let go and just trust that God was looking out for me and planting the seeds to guide me away from my great longing for my mother's love and affection. You see, we can only see what is in front of us and behind us, God can see everything all around us and the future hurts we could and would go through taking different paths which we weren't meant to take. However, we all have free will to do as we choose. I have made many poor choices in my life that make me cringe when I think of them. For many years I did not resist the temptations that were in my path. I was extremely promiscuous. I realize after many years of therapy that being exposed to sex at such a young and vulnerable age gave me horrible cravings and addictions to sex.

I made many terrible decisions because of it.

The guilt continued to plague me and reinforce in me what an awful person I was, and it just about destroyed me. Somehow God always had his hand on me and would always put me on the right path when I would go astray. If you are at a time in your life where you are making poor decisions, God can and will help you too. God can heal everything if you have faith, and you believe.

I have now chosen to walk the path that God leads me to.

I pray that one day you will be brave enough and trust God enough to do the same for yourself.
If there are people in your life that are not safe for you or your children to be around, then do not be around them. God will fill your lives with the right people that he wants to be your family.

The nurse came in and turned off all the machines that were keeping my grandfather alive. What a gift that I could be there alone in the room with the two loves of my life. I am forever grateful that I was in that room with the two of them. I am so happy that my grandma was not alone and that I was at her side as she was always at mine.
Later that night all our family came to be at the hospital together. The waiting room was filled with mostly our family. We were taking turns going into our grandfather's hospital room to read to him. We were reading one of my grandfather's favorite books to him, "Old Man and the Sea," by Ernest Hemingway. Grandpa was an avid reader, and he had a passion for reading anything and everything.

One of the times I was in the waiting room with our family, I was standing off to the side near the doorway in front of the small waiting room when a man and a woman came up to me. I had obviously been crying a lot, my eyes and nose were swollen, and I was doing everything in my power to keep it together. They had a calm and peacefulness about them that I cannot really explain but I will do my best. The woman did all the talking. She told me that they had been watching me for some time and noticed how close I was to my grandma. She told me that they could see a lot of love between the two of us and that it was very beautiful. She told me that my grandma was very lucky to have me and that I was very lucky to have her. She proceeded to tell me that the kind of love that we shared was very rare and special. As my eyes filled with more tears, I agreed with her. She handed me a little blue pebble that had the word, "Peace" on it. I didn't understand that she was giving it to me because my head was so stuffy and confused. She told me that it was for me to keep. I told her thank you and she hugged me, and I said goodbye and walked away.

I walked over to one of my family members and showed the pebble to one of my cousins and turned to show her who gave it to me (It was literally less than 2 minutes). The man and woman that had come to me were no longer there. I need to mention that the exit where the elevators were located was on the complete opposite side of the hospital area where we were standing. I looked everywhere to try to find them, but I never found them. Another odd thing was that not one of my family members saw me talking to them.

I believe to this day that God sent me angels to help me through one of the hardest times I have ever gone through. My heart was so heavy before I met my angels but ever since they started talking to me, there was a calmness to me that I cannot explain.

I believe that God comes to us when we need him,

sometimes we are so busy in this world that we fail to see his many attempts at sending us help.

If you look back at your life at the times you needed him most, think about the people that helped you or the phone call you received that gave you some hope or help.

God is there at every corner of your life. The ones that are bright and filled with happiness and love and the ones that are dark that are filled with sadness, despair, and fear. God never leaves us; we often leave him, and it feels like he has left us.

Sometimes we make poor choices in our lives, and we don't want to believe he is there watching us make so many mistakes, so our shame pushes him away. But I can promise you that he is there through all of it. He is loving you no matter what path you are on. He wants you to need him, to lean on him and believe that he is there to love you despite the poor choices you are making in your life.

The following is a poem that I made up for my grandfather after he died and I read it aloud at his funeral:

Dear grandpa,

I said my "Goodbye's to you today, I knew you wouldn't mind.

We had many loving years between us, those of a treasured and everlasting kind.

It was time to let you go to be with the one who loves you more than grandma or I, it was time *my dear grandpa to let your soul soar high.*

*High above the pain and sorrow of this earthly place, grandpa
I will never forget the constant smile on your face.*

*I'll remember the laughter, I'll remember the
tears, I'll remember countless old movies watched
with grandma and you throughout the years.*

*I know I don't need to remind you of how much you were loved
by me, because we both lived it daily and our love was plain to see.*

All my Love,

Love Your Princess

When someone you love dies, I believe that God puts someone else in your life for you to love and to love you back.

The first time this ever happened to me was right after my grandfather's funeral.

It was my ex-husband's weekend to have the kids, but he and my children went to my grandfather's funeral anyway because my ex-husband had a lot of love and respect for both of my grandparents. After the funeral my ex-husband took the kids home to his house for his week to have my kids, which meant I was going to be alone on a week that I really wanted and needed my kids to be with me.

However, God had other plans...

After the funeral I went back to my grandma's house by myself, and I was extremely sad.

I was sitting on the couch in my grandfather's den with some of my second cousins. One of my cousin's daughter's (Grace) kept teasing me (*mercilessly I might add*). I felt like she was picking on me especially because I was so down and depressed. This went on for the entire day until I left my grandma's house.

This was the beginning of the new person that God put into my life that day for me to love and to love me back. I ended up taking my cousin Grace home with me for the rest of the weekend and a beautiful and long-lasting close-knit relationship started and has flourished into one of my closest relationships to date.

That weekend I opened up and I shared with Grace a side of myself that at that point in time I rarely ever shared. I told her the truth about my father, and she shared personal things with me as well and a close bond was formed between us.

The week after the funeral, I was driving around trying to find brokers' offices to cold call, when I couldn't see well enough from crying too much and it wasn't safe for me to continue driving. I pulled over to a parking lot and let go of all the tears and hurt I was trying to keep inside. I missed my children that I shared 50/50 custody with my ex-husband, and it wasn't my week to have them at the time. I felt so lost and alone, so discouraged with the new job I had just started because I couldn't comprehend my work.

It was as if my brain had shut down because I was too

depressed over the death of my grandfather and the finality of my marriage. I did what I often did at times when I felt sad, I called my grandma.

My grandma answered the phone right away. I was trying to disguise the fact that I had been crying but I couldn't sneak past the one person in the world who knew me.

She asked me what was wrong, and I couldn't keep the tears inside, so I told her everything as usual. I told her that I didn't know how I was ever going to be able to support my children because I was having such a difficult time learning how to do my job. At this point in my life, I had never had any jobs that dealt with using my brain so much. I didn't understand why I was in a job of finance. I never understood how God could use me to help people and lead people to him when my job was about money. I had prayed so hard that God would put me in a job where I could help people. *I felt like God wasn't listening to me.*

I felt so lost in my job and in my life. I felt like God forgot about me and I was struggling to stay afloat in my life. I will never forget what my grandma told me.

She asked me, "Mija, (A spanish word that means: my daughter or a form of endearment) when you build a building where do you start building first?" I wasn't sure at the time where she was going with this, but I said, "At the bottom?" She said, "Yes, you start at the bottom, brick by brick." She proceeded to tell me that now, I was just starting with my building of learning my new job and I was just on the first brick. She said that right now everything was so new that nothing was familiar to me but that brick by brick I would learn it and build my whole building and that one day I would be at the top of the building looking down.

I need to tell you that at the time that I was going through all of this, it seemed so far out of my reach but that day, my grandma gave me hope.

Less than a year later, I called my grandma and told her that I was on top of the building...

A couple years after that, I had my twelve-year-old daughter with me, and I went into the office I worked at when my manager asked my daughter to come look at something on some papers he was reading. He asked her to find my name on the paper and to tell me what number was next to my name. She said, "number one."

I had no idea what documents he was reading but he proceeded to tell my daughter that I was number one in the retail division of the entire company including the whole East and West Coast.

To say the least, I learned brick by brick.

You may be at the beginning of a new job, a new marriage, newly divorced, the loss of a loved one or many other hard places in your life. We all start at the beginning or on that first brick of difficult parts of our lives and with constant prayer and God at our side, we will come through it stronger than we were before we started.

CHAPTER 13

Mortgage Industry

As I told you before, I questioned why God would put me into the industry of Finance when all I wanted was for him to use me and the gifts that I had to use to help people.

At the time, I didn't have a financial bone in my body.

God is funny that way, he uses us in ways we would never begin to understand or choose for ourselves, because he is God, and he knows all. It really doesn't matter if we understand, all that matters is if we are willing to be used for God's good and his glory.

I had always wanted him to use me to help people since I was a small girl. I still want him to use me. I will want him to use me to help people long after he has taken me from this world.

I am a planner; I always need to have a plan. It helps me to function; it lessens my stress and gives me the illusion of control over things in my life. I am well aware that I do not ever have control. Control is in the hands of my maker, and I know this, but I still try to make myself feel as if I have as much control as possible. *I am sure it comes from not having control of so many important things in my childhood and early adulthood.*

Knowing that I was getting divorced I had already started applying to at least 20 different kinds of job positions.

One of the women at my church that I didn't know very well but that was in a Bunco group that I started called me one day because she had heard that I was getting a divorce. She surprised me when she said that her husband wanted to talk to me. I didn't know her husband and had no idea why he would want to speak to me (Most people at the church I had gone to knew who I was because I was extremely involved in a lot of different ministries at my church). Apparently, the husband of the woman I knew from Bunco knew who I was because he noticed how active I was in our church. He told me his name and then proceeded to tell me that I should come work at the company that he worked for. He said that I would be great at doing what he did. The company he worked for was a bank and he was a Mortgage Consultant/Loan Officer. I thanked him for thinking about me but told him that I already had a bunch of interviews. He made me promise if they didn't work out to call him. So, I promised him, thinking that I would never need to call him. I didn't want to work in anything that had to do with finance. How could God use my gifts in that kind of career?

About a month later, I would end up calling him and asking him if I could apply with his company because all my interviews and other connections did not pan out.

I was very discouraged and the call I made to him was when I was at my weakest point.

He set up an interview with his boss and I remember his boss talking about all the different job possibilities that I would be good at. I told him that I knew nothing about finance and that I wanted to start at the bottom so that I could learn everything I needed to learn so that I could learn it well. Starting at the bottom meant working a 9:00-6:00 shift behind a desk with my children in daycare. The boss of the guy that referred me told me that he knew that I would be great at being a Mortgage Consultant and that I would have the freedom to stay home with my children and work around their schedule. I had no idea what a mortgage was or what a loan officer did, but I agreed to think about it.

A few weeks later I was at the Christmas party for the Bunco group and the husband of the woman I knew pulled me aside and asked me why I hadn't contacted his boss yet. I told him that I wasn't ready to move forward because I knew that I needed time alone with my kids after the divorce to help them adjust better. He advised me to call his boss and tell him that, so when I was ready that door would remain open for me. *That was great advice.*

I am happy that I took his advice because if it hadn't been for me calling and explaining this to his boss, nine months later when I had to get a job, that door would have been closed.

I believe that everything happens for a reason, but of

course at this certain time in my life all I could see was my pain from all the loss I was going through.

I had so much loss to mourn. The death of my grandfather, the loss of my marriage, the loss of my life being with my kids 24/7 and when I needed my church most, eventually I lost it as well because of one insecure priest.

I ended up leaving the Catholic church because I was told by that priest that I was a sinner now that I was getting divorced, and he forced me to resign from every board and every position that I volunteered at the church. *There were a lot of positions for me to resign from.* In the end, I lost my church and all the closest relationships I had ever had up to that point in my life with the people at my church.

To say the least, I was devastated.

I had no idea why I wasn't allowed to volunteer my time; I was extremely angry and hurt by that priest. I left that church and never told any of my friends and other members that went there why I left. I just disappeared from all the people that I had once felt so close to.

I believe that God puts people in our lives for seasons. Depending on how long they are needed. Some people just pass through our lives for a moment but either something they say or something they do makes them an important piece of our lives or something we say or do was needed in their lives. Others are meant to be with us for a long time to fulfill their purpose in our lives and for us to fulfill our purpose in their lives.

In September of 2003, I started my new job as a

Mortgage Consultant. It was an extremely scary
time for me.
As I said before, I had just started working for the bank
and my new position as a Mortgage Consultant for about
a week or two when my grandpa had a stroke at dialysis
on September 16, 2003, and went into a coma.
I was still mourning the loss of my marriage from the
father of my two small children. I had already been
forced to stop all my volunteer work and resign from
all the positions as board member for many of the
committee's that I volunteered for.
I felt lost and alone in the world and then my
grandpa died.

To say the least it was getting hard for me to stay positive
and to learn all I had to learn to be successful in my
new career.

But I had to keep moving forward and do my best
because my children were depending on me.

I knew that I was lucky to have this job especially
because I knew once I got the hang of it and understood
what I was doing I could take my kids out of childcare
and work around their schedule.

I sent out a lot of flyers scared out of my mind every time
my phone rang because I had no idea what a mortgage
was let alone how to help anyone that needed one.

Thankfully, I met this seasoned Mortgage Consultant in
my office that would later become a close friend.
Daisy seemed like an angel to me. An angel that God

sent down to help me and take under her wing. I am sure she had no idea how lonely I was or how isolated I felt in a workplace that I felt like I didn't fit into.

She taught me how to fill out a loan application, she taught me the terms I needed to know to discuss mortgages with potential clients. She basically taught me everything I needed to know about being a Mortgage Consultant. If it wasn't for Daisy helping me and becoming my mentor, I would have not been successful in the mortgage business. Not only did she help me learn how to be a Mortgage Consultant, but she also ended up being a safe haven for me at work and outside of work.

She invited me to go out to lunch with her and other people in our office. She was always so kind, warm and inviting. Unlike a lot of people that worked in our office. We worked in a very cutthroat world but that was not at all how Daisy was. I soon found out that she was a Christian so we would often talk about God. She would often call me her Catholic Christian friend. Later she and her husband would invite me to their church, go with me to Christian concerts and she even invited me to her sister's home for Thanksgiving one year because she knew I was going to be alone.

I am so grateful to Daisy for welcoming me into her world of mortgages and especially grateful for her love and friendship.

Little by little, or brick by brick, I started learning how to be a Mortgage Consultant and more about the mortgage industry. I started adding a little bit of me to my job (like making thank you cards and Holiday cards and *sending them to my clients and potential clients).* Once I added a bit of me into my job, I felt more comfortable with my job and felt more comfortable in what I was doing.

One day, I received a call from an unhappy man that needed to refinance his existing mortgage. I was scared to death, but I did the best I could unconfidently. It didn't help that the man was very crabby and not so nice. I remember asking him if he wanted to meet with me in person or if he wanted me to send him the form to fill out and have him send it back to me or if he wanted me to fill it out over the phone. He ended up wanting me to send him the form in the mail.

I remember one of my coworkers telling me that he would never send it back to me and that I had lost the deal.

I sent the man the form and a return envelope with a note I wrote him.

I had two other customers that called me from my flyers that ended up doing refinances. *I made sure not to give them an option of mailing them the form.* One day, I got a package, and it was in fact the first guy I spoke to about the loan. He had filled out the paperwork I had sent him and was moving forward with the loan process. I called him as soon as I received his documentation. He was always so crabby and mean but I was used to speaking to people that were mean. As time went on, I received more customers that I did loans for and gained a lot more confidence. For some reason or another the first guy's loan took forever because there were so many problems.

One day he called and made the girl that answered the phones cry. At that point, I had finally had enough. I was so mad that when he answered I said something I knew he didn't expect to hear. "Hello Mr. So and so, can I ask you a personal question?"

"Uh, I dunno, I guess." "What is hurting you?" "What?" *Angry voice.* I said, "Something really has to be hurting you for you to be so mean to someone you don't even know and that only answered the phone." Silence…and then a man crying into the phone. "Mr. So and So, are you okay?" More crying.

"Everything is going to be okay; you can talk to me about anything, I am here to listen."

One thing I didn't tell you is that I prayed over every mailer that I sent out. I asked God, please send me anyone you want me to help, emotionally, physically, mentally, or financially.

That client of mine proceeded to tell me that he had to refinance his house to get his wife off his house because his wife was a drug addict and that if he didn't get her off of the house, he was going to lose it. He had two small children, and he was very much in love with his wife. He was at his wits end, and he was so lost.

I asked him, do you believe in God? "He said no, not really." He said that he thought there was a God just not for him. I asked him if he wanted to save his marriage and his wife, and he said yes. I told him to get down on his knees and start talking to God and get down on his knees talking to God every day and that I believed that

God could and would heal anything or anyone as long as he believed.

As time went on, the owner of the escrow company that I used called me and couldn't believe the change in Mr. So, and So. She said she had to call him because there were problems with getting a hold of the wife to sign off on removing her from the mortgage. She couldn't believe how kind, patient and understanding Mr. So and so was. She said it was like she was speaking to a different person and asked me why he was so different. I told her that he was different because he believed in God now.

Everything ended up working out with Mr. So, and So. He met me for lunch after his loan closed and I took him a plaque that had the Footprints prayer on it and I also took him the book by Max Lucado, Traveling Light. I wrote inside the book about God being at his side no matter where he was in his life.

That client called me throughout the years to update me on how he and his family were doing. He ended up getting his wife into a rehab in Hawaii and she was in recovery. He and his family started going to church and made prayer a part of their lives.

Mr. So and so was just the beginning in the many ways God started to use me to help others and lead them to have a relationship with him.

I believe that all the loss and rejection I had at this terrible time in my life was to prepare me and to make room for all

I had to do. Making more time for my children, for learning my new career to make the money to financially support my children and give me the opportunity I needed to be exposed to so many different people that didn't know God.

I shared this story with you to show how God can use you wherever you are. It doesn't matter if you are in a place, you think God cannot use your gifts. Trust me when I say, God will use you to help those around you if and when you are ready and willing to be used to do his work. It doesn't matter where you are. Most of the time, he uses our weaknesses and not our strengths. When I started to understand that God was using me in many ways to help people, I got more confident in the job I was paid to do, and I was very quick to notice when people needed help other than loans. God answers our prayers, sometimes it's not in the way we expect or in the timeframe we want. I pray that you grow wherever you are planted in life, and you reach out and help those around you.

THE FOOTPRINTS PRAYER

One night I had a dream...

I dreamed I was walking along the beach with the Lord, and across the sky flashed scenes from my life. For each scene I noticed two sets of footprints in the sand; One belonged to me, and the other to the Lord. When the last scene of my life flashed before us, I looked back at the footprints in the sand. I noticed that many times along the path of my life, there was only one set of footprints. I also noticed that it happened at the very lowest and saddest times in my life. This really bothered me, and I questioned the Lord about it.

"Lord, you said that once I decided to follow you, you would walk with me all the way; But I have noticed that during the most troublesome times in my life, there is only one set of footprints.

I don't understand why in times when I needed you the most, you should leave me.

The Lord replied, "My precious, precious child. I love you and I would never, never leave you during your times of trial and suffering. When you saw only one set of footprints, it was then that I carried you.

—Author Unknown

CHAPTER 14
The Confrontation

My grandmother phoned me on January 21st, 2002, to tell me that my Aunt Cecilia had passed away. Aunt Cecillia was my mother's sister-in-law that was married to my mother's brother. I didn't understand why her death was bothering me so much considering I had virtually no relationship with her and hadn't seen her since I was a small child. Was it guilt that flooded me? Did I feel guilty for not being closer to this woman that was now dead? At first that is what I thought, but later I realized it was something far greater...

I had been going to one-on-one therapy for about a year and a half and I had just completed a hellacious once a week group therapy that lasted 1 year. I had just got back together with my husband. We had been apart for ten months and I had gone through all the excruciating therapy on my own. It was the very beginning of realizing I was not to blame for the abuse that I endured for the entirety of my childhood. The concept that it was not my fault was just starting to sink into my confused and tormented head.

The feeling I thought was guilt for my aunt had passed

and I was left with anger so bitter that I cursed his name
and his very existence...

I realized the feeling that was making me sick to my
stomach was the fact that at any given time "he" could
die. What that meant to me was that I would be stuck
on this earth with no family and the truth that no
one would ever believe. I would be the one left with
unfinished business and no way for the truth to be
confronted if this man cheated me and died before
he was confronted. I had kept my painful childhood
a secret. As I grew up, I pretended it was a nightmare
and not real, even though my whole life and behavior
was affected by it. When I was in school, I learned about
goals and what a goal meant. I had a goal at a very
young age. My goal was to turn 18 so that I could leave
my painful circumstances. I didn't care about money,
food, a roof over my head or any organized get away. I
just had to turn 18. I once mentioned to my father as a
child that I wanted to leave home. He told me that until
I was 18, I would never be able to leave, he told me that
he would hunt me down and find me and it would be
worse for me. This is how my goal began and went into
effect when I turned 18. I counted down the days for
many painful years.
For the first time in my 35 years of life I fully believed that
I was not to blame for the horrifying experiences of my
childhood. I finally realized that if he had hurt his own
child that he could and would harm others. The hardest
thing I would ever do in my life was the journey that I
was about to embark on, and I knew that the only way
I would get through my horrible task was by the faith

and love that I had in the Lord. So, I began to pray for the strength that I knew existed inside of me. It took me a little over a month to figure out this battle that was going on inside of me and a plan to accomplish my goal. I told my therapist what I needed to do and how it came about and before I could meet with her to get a plan, the journey to my healing began...

I always believed that if my mother only knew what I had endured all those painful years growing up she would love me and finally show me love. I had two painful confrontations to go through and I knew that if I didn't confront my mother first that I would surely lose that opportunity, so I asked Steve if he would call my mother and schedule a day and time to meet with her. Steve calling my mom was the only chance I had to see her because she would never agree to see or speak to me. As I was getting into the car to go to my counseling appointment, Steve phoned me from his work telling me that he just spoke to my mother and that she would come meet him at our house right now. I panicked, I wasn't ready, what would I say and how could I do this without the help of my therapist? I had no choice but to get out of my car and call my therapist and cancel my appointment. I was shaking beyond control and my stomach was hurting so badly that I couldn't concentrate. I phoned a friend that was aware of my situation and arranged for her to get my children from school and watch them until I was through with my ordeal. I started praying like there was no tomorrow and it seemed like forever before Steve got home from work. We both sat down on the couch and started to pray together. Before long, my mom showed up and I stayed sitting on the couch while Steve went to open the door. She looked very surprised to see me there, but she said hi to me anyway. I had never been so nervous in my entire life. She sat down on the couch and asked what Steve wanted to speak to her about. I spoke up and told her that it was actually me that wanted to talk to her. I told her that what I was about to tell her was not easy for me to do, that in fact it was the hardest thing I had ever had to do in my entire life. I said, "Mom, do you remember when dad's mom once told you to never leave your daughter alone with your husband?" Silence... "You should have listened to her." I broke down at that point and as I did, I heard her say, "No, he would never do anything like that, he hates that kind of thing." I told her it was true, and she said, "well, if Steve is here, I guess it must be, but it's very hard for me to believe." I told her that I wanted to have a relationship with her, and I wanted her to know my kids and have a relationship with them as well. Meanwhile, her rough demeanor never changed. I told her that I was going to confront my father and believe it or not she voiced concern for my well being. I told her that I confronted her first because I didn't know what he would do. I figured he would lie and do something radical like move you away so that I could never contact you. She said she had to go because he would wonder where she was. She told us not to tell him that we had spoken to her. I didn't understand why she would still be so concerned about him and what he thought but there was nothing to be said at that point except to ask her if he was home now and she said, "Yes, but don't talk to him now because he has workers in the backyard." She left and I had a very strange feeling like nothing had changed. After she left, Steve convinced me to go speak to my father at that very moment because I had already just gone through the beginnings of it. He also liked the fact that there were workers present because he thought it would be safer for me. My father was a very violent man. He had loaded guns throughout the house and we both knew that there was a very high possibility that he would use one of them on me for coming forward and bringing the truth out in the open. For some reason I wasn't afraid. I kept praying that God would be a shield all around me and protect me in every way that I needed protection. I repeated it over and over all the way to my parent's house. At the time, I had never read or heard of the scripture that this came from, but I kept picturing myself wearing a shield of armor that covered my entire body. I believe that day in my desperation The Lord put that prayer on my heart.

Many years later I came across the scripture **Ephesians 6:13-17, FULL ARMOR OF GOD:**
Therefore take up the whole armor of God, that you may be able to withstand in the evil day, and having done all, TO STAND FIRM. Stand therefore, having fastened on the belt of truth, and having put on the breastplate of RIGHTEOUSNESS And, as shoes for your feet, having put on the readiness given by the GOSPEL OF PEACE. In all circumstances take up the shield of Faith, with which you can extinguish all the flaming darts of the evil one; and take the helmet of

salvation, and the sword of the SPIRIT. Which is the word of GOD.

This is one of those prayers I pray over everyone I love each day. To protect them from evil in their lives.

I asked God to speak through me and to be with me throughout the endeavor I was about to go through and to not let me be afraid. I knew God would protect me no matter how violent the situation got, and I was ready to die if I had to, to hold my father accountable for his actions. Steve insisted on following me and staying in his car parked down another street, so I let him.
I parked on my parents' culdesac being very aware of not parking too near his house. I was walking up his street when I saw him standing in the arch way of the garage and the backyard near the pool. I saw the workers in the back yard and slowly my father felt my presence and turned around to face me as I was walking up his driveway. He looked at me and acted like I was his long-lost daughter that had come home. He came over to hug me and I had my arms crossed and dodged his hug. *There was no way this man would ever touch me again.* I asked him if my mother was home, and he said no. Then I asked him if I could speak to him. He had a strange look on his face and said, "Yes." He motioned for me to go through the garage into the house and was planning on following me and I just stood there waiting for him to pass first. I strategically placed myself where I had the control, I would never again be left dominated into ugly and terrifying situations. As I followed him into his house that filled me with fear, he asked what I

wanted to talk about. I had no idea what I was going to say because I had not planned a speech or any of what I needed to say. I trusted that God would move me to speak from my heart when he was ready and he did...I said, "I think we both know why I am here." His eyes got huge, I asked if we could sit down in the other room, and he said yes. Again, I strategically placed myself. I started to speak and the first words out of my mouth were.

"The Truth Shall Set You Free!" I told him that I was here to forgive him for physically, emotionally, and sexually abusing me throughout my childhood." He shocked me by crying and telling me that he had wanted to speak to me about it and almost came over to my house many times. He immediately made the whole thing all about himself and how much he has suffered all these years. He stated that he went to Rome and confessed it to a bishop and the bishop asked him if he was sorry and he said yes, and the bishop told him that he was forgiven. He continued not thinking for one moment about me and any pain that I endured. He continued putting all the focus on himself and how miserable he was, which was usual for him. Not once did he apologize to me or ask me how it affected me and my life. His only concern was to manipulate me into feeling sorry for him. Which of course did not work.

I was losing my patience with him and realized I had so many questions I needed to have answered and he was wasting my time and filling me with annoyance. I told him, "How dare you hurt that innocent little girl." *I was referring to myself.* I then asked him, "Who did it to you?" He got angry and defensive and started yelling at me,

saying that it was none of my business and no one ever
did anything to him. I pushed the subject and said, "I
know someone did it to you, who was it?" He finally said,
yes, that someone had done it to him but that it was
none of my business. I said, "None of my business? You
better believe it's my business! For the past 35 years it
has been my business and it has affected every part of
my life and I have a right to know. I told him that I knew
who it was, I told him that it was his own father. He got
very angry and defensive and started freaking out. Why
would his own mother tell my mother to keep her own
son away from me? *I would later find out it was possibly
one of his neighbors when he was a child, not his father/my
grandfather.*

I gained control of my life that Wednesday afternoon.

I realized many things at that moment. One being that
I had one chance to get all the questions that haunted
me for so many years answered in a once in a lifetime
situation. I began by speaking about myself as a young
girl in the third person. I thought it was about time
someone defended my younger self, even if it was me…I
said, "How dare you hold a loaded gun to your head in
front of your thirteen-year-old daughter, threatening
to kill yourself if she ever told anyone." "What kind of
normalcy did your daughter have in living her life? I told
him that he was a coward and that he would never have
killed himself and that he was trying to scare me into
silence, it worked until now. I told him I would never be
silent again and that he needed help so that he would

never hurt any other children. *It took me many years of therapy to finally understand that it was not my fault.*

If you have been sexually abused or abused in any way, I want you to know that it was NOT your fault. You were an innocent child. Let go of the shame and the guilt, it is not yours to carry. God loves you and wants all good things for you. He wants you to carry joy in your heart. Let go of the sadness and anger and give it to God because his shoulders are much bigger than yours.

I asked him if he hurt my younger sister and he said, "no, it was only you. I never hurt anyone else." I didn't believe him and felt anger well up inside of me, but I heard this voice in my head say, "Not now Faith, not now." So, I decided to get some of my other questions answered. I asked him if he had dirtied my name all throughout my childhood so that no one would like me and if I ever told anyone they would not believe me if I came forward with the truth. He said, "Yes, yes, I did." I asked him if he brainwashed my brothers and my mother so that I was left with no one in my life, and he confessed this to be true. I asked him if he pushed me away every time, I begged him to be my father and love me because he saw me to be a good person and couldn't stand to see me because then it made him feel guilty for what he had done to me. I also asked if he kept me out of his life so that he could believe that I was a bad person and then he could believe that I deserved it. He said yes. I had 35 years to make sense of my messed-up life and I had one afternoon to get the truth and gain clarity from my father. I started to realize something as I heard that haunting voice from my past saying, "I am going to kill myself." Honestly, it was music to my ears to hear him say that because it was exactly what he said to me when I was thirteen years old. I wasn't crazy, I wasn't mistaken, he really did put a loaded gun to his head when I was thirteen years old. I really did take the loaded gun away from my father's head after crawling to his room after being kicked all over my body with his steel toed shoes and waking up after he kicked me in the head until I was unconscious. I knew my father would finally kill himself that day if I didn't do something about it, but what was I to do? As I watched this mouse of a man sobbing like a small child in the chair, I was amazed at the fact that almost everyone who knew my father was intimidated by him. He was extremely respected in the business world and wasn't afraid of anyone that I was aware of. However, that day I realized he was afraid of the truth... it is amazing how the truth really does set a person free. The fear I had all my life left me completely that day. I realized as I watched my father cry and say over and over that he was going to kill himself that I was free to live my life now and to always tell the truth. I wasn't about to let my father kill himself this day or any other so I did what anyone else would have done in my situation and that was to get reinforcements. I told this small child that sat in my father's chair that I needed to get something out of my car that I really needed to give to him. I played on the present remorse that my father displayed (whether it was fake or real I will never know) and told him to stay in the chair until I got back. He said he would wait. I never saw a human being so insane in front of me before that time or after that day, but I took him at his word that he would wait to kill himself until after I returned. I went out the front door running like a lunatic myself and crying the whole time to tell Steve to come help me. I was afraid my father was watching me out of one of the front windows of the house, so I was waving my arms to Steve to come to me. He thought it was a getaway that I needed so he started his car. I was waving frantically trying to tell him not to drive but to come with me into the house. I ran back to the house mouthing to him from a distance to come into the house from the opened garage. I went into the house through the front door and my father was still in the same chair hunched over. I realized Steve hadn't gone into the house yet, so I had to tell my father that I forgot my keys and that I needed to go back outside. I really had forgotten my keys and my phone was in the car and my original plan was to call Steve on his phone and tell him to come into the house because my father was going to kill himself. So, I started to go out of the garage to get Steve. I opened the door to find him waiting because he didn't know what was going on. I brought him into the house and informed him in front of my father that my father was going to kill himself. In this strange and psychotic voice my father said, "I am not going to kill myself." Steve looked at me like, what did you do with your father and who is this man sitting in this chair. Steve sat down on the couch across from the one I sat on, and my father began his sad sob woe is me routine. "I didn't mean to hurt anyone, I confessed to a bishop in Rome, and he told me I was forgiven, I am not a monster." I realized that Steve felt sorry for him. For a moment in the beginning of our conversation, I did too. But the way my father recited every word as if it were a play or a movie, I realized that again my father was trying to manipulate the situation as well as its participants. I told my father that I was going to tell my brothers that he was a pedafile and that my Aunt Hildi and Uncle Stanley already knew. I told him I was going to keep him away from all children and that he needed to get help and he said it was only me and that he was fine and didn't need any help. He proceeded to tell me that I couldn't tell anyone else.

At that moment, he got up and walked to the stairs as if he was going to go up and I said, "Where do you think you are going?" He said, "I have to use the restroom." I said, "then use the one downstairs, you've got to be kidding if you think I am going to come this far and let you kill yourself before I confront you in front of my family." He said, "I am not going to kill myself." I said, "You better believe you're not going to." My father went to the downstairs bathroom and the look on Steve's face told me a lot. For the first time in my life, I felt like Steve respected me. He looked me in the eyes and said, "I have never seen you like this before. I cannot believe how strong you are."

It wasn't my strength, it was the power of God speaking through me, protecting me, and making me strong like one of his warriors. Honestly, I could never have done any of what I did that day without him and the faith he blessed me with.

My father came back and sat down in the chair and

at that point my mother walked in from the garage door. I immediately got up and whispered that he had admitted what he had done and that now he said he was going to kill himself.

My mother was very uncomfortable with the whole idea of me being in her house and I am sure she was fearful that my father would find out that we already spoke to her. She kept up her game of not knowing and decided to keep herself busy in the other room to not be involved with the uncomfortable discussion we were having. My father sat up in his chair and gained control of himself and when she was out of earshot, he told us he wasn't going to kill himself to not say anything to my mother because it would kill her if she knew. I said, "I won't tell her, but you will." He said, "No, I am not going to tell her anything!" I gained control of the entire situation and I said, "Oh yes you are! I didn't go through 35 years of pain for you to get away from facing the truth." I called my mother into the room we were in, meanwhile my father was begging me not to say anything. My mother came into the room, and I told her that my father had something to tell her. She was acting like she didn't know what was going on and my father finally said in a confident voice, "When Faith was a child, I used to abuse her." That wasn't good enough for me, so I said, "How did you abuse me?" He started to raise his voice and try to dominate me by putting fear into me, but it didn't work on me anymore because I wasn't a child anymore. I guess he realized it as well because he told her that he physically, emotionally, and sexually abused me.

My mother's response was well acted out, I felt as if I

was watching a play or in that case, I was in one of my nightmares. "Oh Damian." My father immediately went into his drama about how much he had suffered and how he told the bishop in Rome, and he was forgiven but that he constantly was in pain. Blah, blah, blah. To my dismay, my mother got up and walked across the room to where my father sat. She then wrapped her arms around him and kissed him and told him that we all make mistakes. She then went upstairs and got a book of prayers and started reading out of it. Was this really happening or was I imagining all of this? Wasn't I supposed to finally be hugged and loved by my mother? This was all wrong, it wasn't at all what I had imagined and hoped for. I felt cheated again and this made no sense at all to me. Was I alone in the fact that it was me that had been wronged and that I was the victim not my father? I decided that this whole scenario wasn't working for me and so I went on to the next thing that popped into my mind. I told my father that it was time for him to tell my brothers. He said, "No, you can't make me do that!" My mother even told me that it wasn't necessary and that no one else had to know. She said that it could just be our secret.

I felt I was reliving a nightmare, she wanted me to continue to keep the horrible secrets of my childhood and pretend like it never happened. How could a mother say that to her child? I didn't understand. When my mother made her comments, it put me over the edge, and I yelled at my mother and told her to get my brothers on the phone immediately and get them over here as soon as possible. She immediately got up and my father said, "No Martha!" I looked her in the eye and said, "Do not listen to him and get my brothers on the phone, NOW!" She did what I said and phoned both of my brothers. By that point my father was pleading with me to not make him tell my brothers. I said, "Fine, I will give you a choice, you can tell them together or you can tell them separately." He chose separately. So, I had my mother call one of my brothers back so that the two of them wouldn't arrive at the same time. When my brother Arnold got there, he was very surprised to see me because he hadn't seen me in my parents house in a very long time. He gave me a hug and proceeded to sit down on the couch next to me. He had a puzzled look on his face like he was wondering what was going on. My father was sitting straight up in his chair by this point ready for his performance, looking as if he had everything in his control and with his normal controlled voice said, "I have gotten everyone together today because there is something I need to tell you." *Okay, to say the least I was very angry because yet again this man is still thinking he is in control of the situation and trying to make it look like he is in charge.*

Of course, I couldn't keep my big mouth shut anymore, so I said, "Excuse me, who got everyone together today?" My father was clearly annoyed because I was correcting him and bringing it to my brother's attention that he was not in control of the situation. He reluctantly said, "Well Faith got us together." He then moved forward in this melodrama and told my brother that he abused me when I was young. I said, "How did you abuse me?" He said, "I emotionally, physically and sexually abused your sister when she was growing up." My brother just looked down and my father started his acting lessons again, repeating the same things that I was getting tired of hearing. "I told a bishop in Rome, and he forgave me. I am not a monster, I had to live with this my whole life, I know I was wrong, I would cut off my right arm if it would take away what I've done." Blah, blah, blah.

I will never forget what my brother said next, he turned to me as I was sobbing and told me, "You have no idea how strong of a person you are." All the while, my mother was busy pointing out that we all make mistakes, and my father was only human. At this point my brother Arnold starts saying how he is not perfect and that he has made many mistakes in his life and that we do all make mistakes. While I was sitting there, I couldn't understand why everyone was feeling sorry for my father when I was the innocent one. Later of course I realized many painful facts.

The doorbell rang and I had to take a deep breath because my hero was finally there, and I hadn't seen him in many years. It was my eldest brother Tommy, who was told by my mother and father that I was a horrible person. I loved my brother more than any words could possibly express. He was my hero, he never hurt me, he was the only one that ever showed me kindness in my immediate family. He used to do gymnastics with me in the living room with his long skinny legs flying all over the room. He would make me laugh by the silly things he did. I loved Tommy and all these years he had no idea why. That soon changed. He walked into the room and looked at me like he was relieved to see me there as well as being surprised. I got off the couch and ran to him and we hugged each other for what seemed to be a very long time. He looked at me and said, "This is so weird because I was thinking about you a lot lately, and I was going to try to find you." He looked at everyone in the room, almost sizing up the situation and not being able to make sense of it. He sat down on the couch right next to me. Meanwhile, my father had miraculously regained his composure because of my eldest brother being there that I couldn't even say a word. I had my head down and sheer terror flooded my body as my father proceeded to tell the one person, I adored that he physically, emotionally, and sexually abused me while I was growing up. I could not stop sobbing. I was so ashamed of what I had gone through all my life and the fact that my brother Tommy finally knew it put me over the edge. I felt like I was in the middle of a nightmare and there was no way I could wake up. My mother started up again about how we all make mistakes, and I just couldn't handle the anger and pain that surged through my body and out of my mouth. I looked up at my mother and said, "How dare you not do your job, you failed me, you failed to protect me and keep me safe." I have been alone all my life with no family (at that point I lost control of my emotions and in shame I closed my eyes and bent over and sobbed like I have never sobbed before). All I heard was the most beautiful voice I had ever heard; it was the voice of my hero fighting for me. The words I heard were, "YOUR NOT ALONE ANYMORE!"

As he swept me up into his arms and held me

as if he was protecting me from the evil that surrounded the room.

My brother stood by me that day. He had a lot to lose to stand at my side, but he chose to stand by what was right and stand against evil.

Later that day my brother came over to my house and he told me that he was sorry but that he thought that my mom had to have known what was happening to me all those years growing up. I told him that what he said was probably true but just for that day, I wanted to believe that she didn't know. I promised him that the next day when I woke up and before I put my feet on the ground that I would admit the truth to myself. But for that one day I needed to believe that she didn't know.

The truth is that I will never really know.

A few days after the confrontation my brother went to his office and my mom was there. She told my brother that Damian hadn't slept in two days and that he wasn't eating. I guess she was really upset about it and trying to make my brother feel sorry for him. However, it didn't work, and my brother told her, "How many nights do you think Faith went without sleep or food?" My mother didn't say anything and changed the subject.

Believe it or not, it still hurts for me to think about that. Many years ago, I found out from an aunt that she witnessed my father beating my mom when my aunt was a young girl. I never knew that he beat my mom too. When they fought, we hid in our rooms. We heard a lot of noises and things being thrown, but I personally never witnessed him hit my mom.

A few years back my sister told me that she called the police on my father because he was beating our mom. The police came but Damian talked his way out of it and my mom backed him up.

I realize now that my mom was a prisoner in her marriage and in her life. She couldn't fight for me because she couldn't even fight for herself. I wonder if she would have been able to fight for me if she wasn't so sick...I guess I will never know and that needs to be okay. All I can do is move forward and let go of the hurt, the anger, and the disappointment. I am thankful that I made it out of that household alive and that I was blessed to have my own family.
A family I was able to keep safe and protect from all the violence and ugliness.

CHAPTER 15
Letter to Family

Dear Family,

I hope this letter finds all of you well. As you all know I spent almost a week at Aunt Hildi and Uncle Stanley's house. On my last evening with them, Uncle Stanley, Aunt Hildi and I stayed up until very early the following morning discussing the very uncomfortable topic of my past. In talking to Uncle Stanley and Aunt Hildi it was brought to my attention that by sharing my traumatic past with you I have also shared a heavy burden with all of you. The word obligation came up in most of our conversations. I did not realize the consequence of my openness in sharing my life with you. If I had known that each one of you would be filled with obligations, I would have never told anyone of you. For each one of you there was a different reason in my sharing my story with you. Aunt Melissa, Uncle David, Uncle Antonio, and Aunt Becky, I had Aunt Hildi and Uncle Stanley tell you because I wanted to keep your children safe. I told my cousins Manuel and Isabella because they had reached out to me for many years and each time they did, I said my polite thank you but always kept my distance. However, on the day of grandpa's funeral, (to be exact at

the reception) my cousin Manuel came to me and asked
if he could speak to me. We went outside and my cousin
fought for me without his knowing. He told me that
he did not know what was going on with my parents,
he only knew that we weren't speaking. He pulled me
outside to tell me that he was on "my side." I realized at
that moment that I wanted to tell him about me and
why I was always so aloof with him and everyone else. I
realized that Uncle Octavio and my cousin Sarah have
also been informed of my history.

Now, I would like to tell you why I told grandma...quite
honestly, I never wanted to tell grandma, just as I never
wanted to tell grandpa, but you see grandma is the
one person that I have shared myself with and the one
person I felt safe with. I told grandma everything I did,
both good and bad and for some reason she still loved
me. I never wanted to tell grandma the truth about me
because I didn't want to hurt her.

However, the last time I was alone with grandma and
grandpa we were in the hospital. It was the day that we
were all at the hospital because it was the day, we all
said goodbye to grandpa. Aunt Hildi and Uncle Antonio
had left to make the arrangements for grandpa's funeral
and grandma, and I stayed alone with grandpa.
Grandma and I were sharing some special moments
with grandpa, and he even took my bracelet off to tease
me. It was one of the most special moments I have ever
experienced.

Grandma and I were both holding grandpa's hand at the
same time, and we were praying over grandpa. When
we were done praying grandma looked at me with tears

in her eyes and out of the blue, told me that she knew that when I was ready, I would tell her whatever it was that I was keeping from her. She then told me that she knew that I wasn't letting her be close to me. Somehow grandma knew that I was keeping something from her, and that day troubled me because grandma is the closest person in the world to me. I have thought about that moment for months at a time and one day I realized that if my grandma knew that there was something I was keeping from her then she would never know who she was to me. I could tell that grandma was already hurting because she knows me so well and can tell when any one of us is in pain. She told me that she could always see pain in my eyes. For a long time, I stayed away from her any time I wasn't doing very well because I knew she could see it. I guess I need to back up and bore you with another humiliating fact. Along with many other dysfunctional traits that I possess, not letting people get close to me is something else I do best. I have always loved people and for some odd reason they seem to like me. They tell me all their personal stuff and for most of my life until very recently I would listen but never share anything about myself. This has been a huge problem with all the relationships I have had in my past. Well now all of you know the core reason why I have been so distant. I did not want anyone to know who I was because quite honestly, I was afraid to know who I was. I have always been aware of the life I went through, I never forgot anything, in fact it was just the opposite with me, I remember everything. Unfortunately for my children, and myself, one day I couldn't pretend all my childhood didn't happen to me anymore.

I was 33 years old, and I couldn't stand being who I was anymore, and I had the closest thing to a nervous breakdown that I had ever had. Steve and I split up. How could I be happy with him when I wasn't happy with myself? Finally, I have come to the point where I need to share with all of you why I told Aunt Hildi and Uncle Stanley. First, I felt completely alone in the midst of my breakdown, and I happened to be at grandma's celebrating Aunt Hildi's birthday 3 years ago exactly on the day of Aunt Hildi's birthday. I don't know why but I asked Aunt Hildi if I could speak to her in grandma's room. I told my Aunt Hildi because aside from grandma I felt closest to her and Uncle Stanley and to be perfectly honest with all of you, I had always wished that she was my mother, and that Uncle Stanley was my father. In all honesty they have acted as good and loving parents would act and if it wasn't for them and for Steve, I probably would not be alive today. My Aunt Hildi and my Uncle Stanley are strong, and I hunger for that. I need strength; however, I have realized over the past 3 years I need my own strength. Only with the strength from surviving my past and facing my future will I find a way to help myself. I want to thank each one of you for your concern and your love. I also want to apologize to those of you who call me, and I do not call back. I am not trying to push any of you away. However, I realize through many hours of tortuous conversations with Aunt Hildi and Uncle Stanley that many of you feel that I have pushed you away. I have not tried to push you away; I am just trying to move forward in my life as a single and working mother of two and face the challenges we all face day to day as well as trying to let my past stay in the past. There is purpose in me bringing forward the truth to all of you and most importantly to myself. There is no doubt that I will always have a heavy burden to carry and many behaviors in which to change but in no way are you to be burdened with any obligation. The best thing any of you can do for me is to pray for me as God is truly the only reason, I am still alive today. It was brought to my attention that some of you are asking Uncle Stanley and Aunt Hildi what you can do to help me. I want you to all know that each one of you has already done it. In hearing my story, in asking how I am doing, in praying for me and by just loving me and accepting me as part of your family. It was also brought to my attention how uncomfortable you are around me and at family gatherings. I must admit that out of all the things we discussed the other night that was the most painful to me. Unfortunately, I don't know what to do about it. Of course, my first reaction is to not be around when there are family gatherings because the worst feeling in the world is in not being wanted. Instead of alienating myself even more, I thought it best to write this letter and address the issues that I have been made aware of. I also want to mention that I am trying very hard to learn to receive love and to trust people. I have not learned either of these things yet, but I am constantly struggling to do so. I have not really had an opportunity to speak with some of you regarding my past and I don't even know if you want to talk about it or not.

I am fine with discussing my past because each time I share my story I do feel stronger. I am not living in my past but as we all know our past helps us to become the person we are today. I need to learn from my past just as each of you needs to learn from yours. I often make the same mistakes over and over, not from lack of trying not to, but with me my therapist used to tell me that I would start on the letter A and once I hit Z the behavior will stop. I know that some of you get frustrated with me and my behavior. Imagine being me, knowing that I do certain things and having to be patient with myself. Unfortunately, I don't learn well from advice from others. I am not saying it isn't helpful in any way, what I am saying is that I guess I am afraid of advice because I am afraid if I do not follow it, either of two things will happen. #1 I will fail and disappoint you and #2 Abandonment, I am afraid that you'll leave me, so I leave first so that it won't hurt so much. I wish for my own sake and for those that are always trying to help me that I did learn easily by advice but unfortunately, I wasn't made that way. Each one of us is made differently, each one with their own quirks and assets. Our uniqueness comes from many different places, the way we were raised does play a part in us, but it is in all of our life experiences compiled together with our hearts that makes us unique to ourselves.

I welcome your love and your prayers. I want you all to know that there was nothing any of you could have done to save me from my childhood and prevent the difficulties I have encountered. There was no way that any of you could have known because I know how to keep a secret. If any of you wish to get together with me to discuss this letter or discuss anything that troubles you, please contact me by email so I won't be caught off guard.

This letter in no way obligates you in any way to respond. I have only invited those of you who need answers to questions you may need to have answered or comments that you need to make. This is a time to be honest and open with your feelings and understanding of where I have been and where I am now. This is a time to grow and to learn and to turn something bad into something good. Again, I ask you to lay down any burdens you may be carrying regarding me and let me carry my own cross. Each day my load gets lighter especially with prayers. I love you all very much. Love, Faith

CHAPTER 16
Cousin Grace

One day, not long ago when my cousin Grace was at my house, somehow this letter came up and my cousin told me about something that I hadn't known but that confirmed the feeling God had put on my heart many years ago.

She told me that after the letter was sent out and received by all the family members that I sent it to; she was at her grandfather's house (who was my uncle) with her mother and father (who were my first cousins) and the topic of conversation was the letter that I had sent out.

My cousin Grace remained quiet and just listened to her parents and grandfather discussing the letter. Grace was already fully aware of what had happened to me during my childhood because I had already confided with her about it on the day of my grandfather's funeral.

Apparently, the immediate response to the letter was anger and my family members wanting to hurt my father for what he had done to me.

They discussed how my father often said very negative things about me to discourage anyone in our family from having relationships with me. My uncle and cousins apparently felt badly because they viewed me as "nutty and different" and believed some of the things that my father had told them.

To be honest, when my cousin told me this, it made me cry. It hurt to hear negative things that people that I loved and respected thought about me.

The odd thing is, I felt the way my family viewed me, but hearing it out loud was quite a different story and still hurts as I am writing this. There are only 3 people on one side of my family that I am hearing about so just imagine what horrible things he must have said to his side of the family and the rest of the friends and family.

Although, knowing how my family viewed me my entire life is an embarrassing thing to tell you, and quite honestly humiliating, I find it necessary to tell the truth as it comes to me so that any of you that feel similarly know that I can relate to you and how you may be feeling.

It really doesn't matter how anyone views me, my actions or what anyone says about me. All that should matter to me is how God views me. I try every single day to be the woman that God created me to be. I fail most of the time, but I know that as long as I keep trying then I am doing the best that I can to overcome my past and all the backlash of it.

CHAPTER 17

Mentoring

One day I was at a friend's house, (her daughter went to school with my daughter, they were both in kindergarten at the time) and I saw an invitation to an open house at a Non-Profit Organization. Apparently, my friend donated money to them, so she was invited to the event. I had never heard of the organization before but that day I found out that it was a nonprofit organization that helped children that were being abused at home and put them into group homes to keep them safe. I asked my friend if I could go with her to the event. When we got there, we sat in some chairs waiting for the event to start. A few young girls around twelve years old sat in front of us and started talking with us. I remember one that was more guarded, but she was funny. One of the other girls was very friendly and very sweet. For some reason the girl that was really guarded gained more of my attention.

My friend and I stayed for the whole open house and after listening to the speaker about what the organization was and finding out it was about keeping kids safe; I became more interested in helping and

volunteering my time. That night, it was put on my
heart to become a mentor for one of the girls. So, I filled
out a form and someone contacted me the next week.
A mentor was assigned to a child to visit, spend time
with and build a relationship with. One day, in the mail I
received the name of the child I would be mentoring, her
name was Tiana.

I contacted the phone number that I was given so that
I could make an appointment to go to Tiana's group
home for my first visit.

The home consisted of about 5 Girls and a house person
that oversaw their care.

When I knocked at the door, I was very surprised to see
the girl that was friendly and sweet that we had seen at
the open house. She ran up and hugged me. I remember
that she wanted affection so badly. However, she was not
Tiana. I came to find out that day that the other guarded
girl that we were speaking to was Tiana. She was very
reserved, she remained guarded, but I could tell that she
was happy that I was her mentor.

In the beginning of my mentorship Tiana would get into
trouble a lot so she would lose privileges, like leaving the
home to go anywhere with me. But after a while, Tiana
opened up and started doing much better. She started
hugging me every time I came to pick her up and when
I left. Every time I came over to visit or pick up Tiana the
other girl would come up and hug me and that created
a lot of jealousy with Tiana. She used to fight with the
other girl a lot and they both would lose their privileges.
At first, I would visit Tiana at the group home but after

a while if she hadn't lost her privileges, I would take
her places. To the mall, to the movies and to my house
with my family. She knew my husband and my two kids.
She would come with us to celebrate different Holidays.
After I got divorced, she would come stay with me on
the weekends and we developed a very close bond. The
more time I spent with Tiana the happier she seemed.
She laughed a lot and that guarded little girl that I first
met wasn't guarded with me anymore.

I was Tiana's mentor until she went back with her mom,
and I had no way of contacting her.

I heard from her only one time after she had turned 18.
She said she was doing well and was living in Texas.

In the end, I am so happy that I could make any kind of
connection with her to help her not feel so alone.

I realize now why Tiana first got my attention, I was also
extremely guarded, and I believe that I saw that in Tiana
so I could relate to her. Mentoring a child that had been
through a lot of the same painful things I went through
as a child was extremely painful to me because at times
when I would see her, I relived my own grief, but it was
also a huge part of my healing. It was a very impactful
time for my own growth and acceptance of who I
was. I realize that if I hadn't gone through my painful
childhood, I would have never been able to understand
Tiana or relate to her and understand her and her
actions the way I was able to. This was really a start
for me understanding how I could use all my darkest
moments for good.

We have all had dark moments in our lives, some more than others. I have learned over the years how important it is to take the pain in our lives and use it to help others. It gives us a sense of purpose to use our broken and hurtful parts of our lives.

CHAPTER 18

Last Chances

On Valentine's Day 2009, I packed up my kids, our two dogs (Star and Rico) and we left at 3:30am to drive out of state 6 hours away to surprise my niece for Valentine's Day. My niece went to live with her mom after her high school graduation in June of 2008 and we missed her. Even though she came out to visit occasionally, it still wasn't enough for my kids and I because we were so close to her. I was also close to my niece's mom Cathy, whom we stayed with when we went to visit my niece. At that time, I had known Cathy for over 28 years which is well over half my life. We had gone through a lot of family drama, and she will always feel like family to me even though she and my brother divorced many years ago.

Well, we arrived safely at my niece's house and our spirits were high because we couldn't wait to see our family. However, when we arrived, I found out that my niece and Cathy were going to be driving back home with us. I thought it was odd considering we just drove over six hours to come see them. Cathy looked at me with a concerned and worried look on her face and she said, "Your brother didn't tell you?" I said no. She told me she would tell me later when the kids weren't around because they were young. I went inside, along with my children and when the kids were in another room, I pulled Cathy aside and said, "Tell me whatever you need to tell me." She proceeded to tell me that my mother called her about a week ago to tell her that she was dying. As harsh as this sounds, my mother was always dying and I cannot even keep count as to how many times we went to the hospital to say goodbye to her, so I didn't get the full effect of the situation until Cathy told me that my mother now had Leukemia from all the radiation and Chemo treatments the doctors had her do to save her from the Lupus. I have no idea how long she did the treatments for but apparently it had been discussed that she would end up developing Leukemia and dying from that but at least it would prolong her life for a few more years from when she started the treatments. She told my ex-sister-in-law that her body was no longer making blood. My niece and her mother were going to drive down to the state where we lived to donate platelets for my mother. Of course, I had no idea about my mother's situation because I hadn't spoken to her in almost seven years. On February 27th, 2009, would be exactly seven years to the day.

I remember the date so well because that was the day the confrontation with my family happened.

Until that point in my life, I had suppressed my pain over the loss of my mom standing by my father's side and not choosing me. However, at that moment I realized that I was on borrowed time, and I had to do something about it before it was too late. What I was going to do, at that moment I had no idea, but I was aware I needed to act on it quickly.

I realize now that if I hadn't eventually acted on these feelings I had at this time, I may have never received any kind of closure or healing.

If you are hesitating about something similar, I urge you to take a leap of faith and trust in the signs that God may be sending you. If you hear God's small voice inside of you telling you to act on something, be brave and act on them because life is short, and moments are fleeting.

CHAPTER 19

Donating Blood

I found out the information from Cathy about where I was supposed to go to donate my blood, so I made an appointment to donate my blood on a Friday. I was supposed to donate my platelets for my mother, but I came down with a migraine headache that was the beginning of the stomach flu. I had the stomach flu the entire weekend and I still did not feel well. I didn't understand why I had to get sick hours before I was going to accomplish something so important, something that would have helped give me closure. I believed that God must have had a good reason. Maybe there were people there that day and time I was supposed to be there that God did not want me to run into. I didn't know, I just had to trust that God knew better than I did. I woke up on that Friday morning at 3:00am with a horrible headache, normally I would have taken some Advil so that I could go back to sleep and when I would have woken up the headache would have been gone. However, when you donate platelets, you cannot have aspirin for 72 hours before donating. I was planning on still struggling through the appointment, but I called my brother, and he told me that the Red

Cross does not want you to donate blood when you are not feeling well. It is a good thing because my migraine got progressively worse and by the time, I got home from dropping off my son to school I got home just in time to get sick in the bathroom.

I believe that there is a reason for everything, especially when things don't make any sense.

I wasn't sure anymore if I should donate blood for my mother because doubt, fear and uncertainty creeped into my mind.

However, a couple of weeks later my brother told me that he heard that our mom was back in the hospital. I got really upset and realized that I needed to donate now. I got on the phone and contacted The American Red Cross. I was trying to schedule an appointment to donate platelets, but they were so booked up that they did not have anything available in the morning for a few weeks. I felt like I may not have a few weeks. The lady assisting me on the phone suggested that I donate my blood because my mom needed blood and no one had donated blood for her in a long time, and they had available appointments to donate blood.

Also, it seemed no one had donated platelets for a couple of weeks. I left an hour later to go donate blood. I don't know if I mentioned my great fear of needles...

I was nervous but I knew it was something I had to do, not for Martha, but for myself.

The nurse that helped me was planted there that day just for me. I know this because she was exactly who I needed to help me. I told her about my great fear of needles and that I have passed out in the past from having blood taken from my finger. Yes, when it comes to blood taking and needles, I am a wimp. Yes, I have had two children by C-Section.

It was funny because for some reason this nurse got attached to me too. Another nurse tried to come in and take over after I was done answering some questions behind closed doors. I was waiting for my nurse and this other nurse came in and was ready to take over, but my nurse kept telling her that she was already taking care of me and that she didn't need any help. My nurse was bugged after the other nurse finally left and after she closed the door she said, "We've bonded, she can't take you away from me." It felt good to have someone I didn't even know defend her time with me. She already understood me. I passed the questions I had to answer to donate my blood and then she pricked my finger so she could test my blood for iron and all the other nutrients she had to check for (No, I did not pass out this time when the blood was taken from my finger). She got excited and happy when she was checking my blood because apparently, I have good blood. I lived through donating my blood, I didn't cry, pass out or get sick. Thank you to my wonderful nurse that truly is in the right profession. She was extremely caring and kind the way a nurse should be. She had a great sense of humor, and we laughed quite a bit. The nurse asked me if it was a friend or family member that I was donating my blood for. I told her the truth; it was for my mother. She said, "Oh how sweet, how is your mom doing?" Before I answered my eyes filled up with tears and I said, "Honestly, I don't really know, I heard she was in the hospital again." She looked sad. I told her that my brother was going to come in and donate soon and that I was going to tell him to ask for her. She looked at some papers on a clipboard and asked me if it was Damian (apparently my father had an appointment the next day). I told her no, that was my father. She called another nurse over and asked her if she knew my father and the nurse said yes and got all happy when she found out I was his daughter.

Apparently, he came to donate platelets every other weekend. I told her it was probably not a good idea to tell him anything about me. My nurse told the other nurse to go away because she wanted to talk to me in private. I told my nurse that I hadn't spoken with my mom in over seven years. She told me I should try to contact my mom and I told her that I had already tried but that she had no interest in seeing me. I never told that kind nurse my story but somehow, I feel in my heart that she knew there was a good reason. My nurse told me that maybe I could send her flowers or something. I told her that I was donating my blood for her and that was the most I could do. The nurse came over and hugged me and her eyes were filled with tears as were mine. She told me that she knew that I was a good person and that whatever happened I did the right thing by coming and donating blood for her. She will never know how healing it was for me to have her as my nurse that day. I don't even remember her name; all I know is that God puts angels in our lives when we most need them, and I believe that nurse was the angel he sent me in my time of need.

If you are going through anything in your life where you are struggling and not knowing what to do, pray and ask God to guide you. If you need to do something that is difficult but something that is right and good, then ask God to give you the strength that you need, and he will give it to you. By the way, the first day that I was supposed to donate blood, I believe my father was there donating blood that day. Everything happens for a reason.

CHAPTER 20

The Need for Closure

I found out that my mom almost died a couple of weeks ago. Apparently, she was sleeping, and she told my father that something was wrong and that she was dying. She told him to call 911 and he did. When they got to the hospital, they found out that her potassium level was too high and if she had come 5 minutes later, she would have been dead. Apparently, all she does is sleep and barely eat. She used to love to read but now she can't even read because she falls asleep the minute she starts reading. Her quality of life is not there. But did she ever really have a quality of life with a husband like my father? I can't help but feel sorry for her and to be honest I feel sorry for myself as well. How sad that she could have had so much more love in her life, instead of protecting and standing by the side of a jealous and insecure pedophile husband.

On April 1, 2009, I was sitting at my desk waiting for my work phone to ring and I looked at the blank pad of paper in front of me and I started writing a letter to my mother...

Dear mom,

I am sorry that you are so sick. I know that you don't want to see me because I called, and your husband told me that you didn't want to ever see me again. I find that extremely hard to understand considering that I was an innocent child that was repeatedly molested by her own father (your husband) for most of my childhood.

I didn't do anything wrong.

I want you to know that I forgive you for not protecting me and for choosing to stand at the side of evil.

I will never understand the choices you have made. Standing beside your husband who is a pedophile and abandoning your position of mother and daughter to a wonderful mother you have and who loved and raised you as her own child. You have made decisions only you can answer to when your day comes, and you stand before the Lord. I pray for you daily as does grandma. We both pray that the Lord would open your eyes, heart, and soul to the truth so that God can forgive you for the horrible choices you have made.

The last thing I ever told you on February 27, 2002, was that I wanted to have a relationship with you, and I wanted you to have a relationship with my children. I told you the ball was in your court. You obviously made your decision and have lived with that decision your remaining years left here on earth.

I want to thank you for the good memories I did have with you as a small child. For putting my hair up in hand rolled curls when your fingers hurt from the soars you had and for buying me paper dolls when you really couldn't afford it. Most of all, I want to thank you for the one night when I was about 4 or 5 years old when we were sitting in my room in the house I grew up in, at my little white table in my room when you talked to me about God and going to heaven. You gave me the biggest gift I ever received and that was you distilling in me about God and about God's love. I want to remind you that despite the poor decisions we make in life, one thing can be certain... God loves you so much mom, despite the decisions that you made.

Innocent people were hurt by your decisions. I think you ended up hurting yourself worst of all. You lost the one person you loved most in this world because you stood up for the side of bad and wrongdoing. You know as well as I do beneath all the brainwashing your husband has put you through, my brother stood up for what was right and good and that was why you lost him. Because you didn't stand where you should have. I am so sorry you have gone through so much physical pain as well as the emotional and spiritual pain you have been going through all this time.

I am also sorry that you didn't have any love in your heart for the daughter that loved you so much and for the grandkids you never got to know.

I miss the mom in you that I knew when I was little, and I know I will always hold a hole in my heart where your love should have been.

I will always be here for you mom, because despite your hurtful decisions towards grandma, my children and me, I still love you.

Love,

Faith

I will never know if my mother ever received, opened, or read my letter. What I do know is that I have peace because I was able to tell her the truth that dwells in my heart and in my mind. I have no control of what others do; all I have control over are the decisions I make. It was my decision to mail the letter I wrote to my mother minutes after I wrote it because it was something I knew that I had to do.

You may be at the point in your life where you need direction. (I visualize a fork in the road where you have the option to go in one direction or another). I have been at that crossroad more times than I can count. If I can be so bold as to suggest that you start praying and asking God for the clear signs that you need to determine which way to go. Ask God for the guidance you need to pursue the healing you rightly deserve. You can never go wrong with the truth, because as it says in the bible, "The truth shall set you free."

CHAPTER 21
Rejection

I called my brother yesterday to see how he was doing. He told me he was on the way to donate platelets for our mother again. He told me a few days ago that he sent her flowers with a card that said if she wanted to see him to call her. She called him the day before yesterday. I am happy for my brother that he doesn't know what it is like to be rejected by our mom. I am happy for my brother that he was able to act on how he felt and that he got a good response to his efforts.

For the first time in my life, I was jealous of my brother.

The week before my brother sent his card and flowers to our mother, my 15-year-old daughter and I went to go see my mom in the hospital. We had to wear special gowns, face masks and gloves because she was so very sick.

I remember that the gowns and everything we had to wear was a light yellow.

My heart was pounding, and I was extremely nervous. My daughter and I went into the room and this tiny lady that I didn't even recognize was laying in the bed. It was my mother...

When we came into the room, she was sleeping but she

opened her eyes. We were very far away from her; we were still near the door when I told her who I was and who Sierra was. She tried scooting away from us and towards the opposite side of the bed. She looked scared and very upset that we were there. She told us that we couldn't be there and that we had to leave right away. My daughter and I immediately left the room, and I was sobbing as we took off the garments that we had put on to go into the room. I cried all the way to my car and couldn't even start driving because I was so upset. It was devastating for me to have my own mother react to our visit like that. Especially knowing that she was dying and didn't have much time left.

The pain and hurt that I felt in my heart cannot be described in words, although I will try to explain. To be rejected, cast aside all my life from the two people in the world that were supposed to love and protect me is so painful that only the person reading this book that has gone through the same pain can comprehend and feel in their heart how devastating it feels. I will continue to write about the pain that dwells in my heart for the sole purpose of the individuals that are reading this book that have never been understood, that have never felt like anyone could ever imagine the pain they hold in their hearts. For the individuals that know the loneliness they can never escape, they too will never be alone, because I understand your pain, I understand the constant loneliness that accompanies you with every step you take in this life. I understand, you are not alone! I am not alone, because we are all together. We understand together the suffering and pain that was not supposed to take place in our lives. It wasn't right what they did to us, it isn't right how they treat us now. We do have a choice to be like them or to be like us. I chose to be like me and to go against everything that they represent a very long, long time ago. I chose to donate my blood to help Martha even though she doesn't want me and even though she may not even use my blood because it was me that donated it. I choose to continue to pray for her and for my father that they would see the truth and the mistakes they have made in their lives and that they continue to make so they can change their ways before it is too late for them. I choose to write a letter and feel the sting of rejections, for the sole purpose of saving my mother's soul. The truth is, I will probably never see my mother again, I will probably never hear a response from her, I will not be invited to her funeral, and I will never have a mom that loves me. I would be lying if I said I didn't care. I would be lying if I said it didn't devastate me beyond words.

However, I know that God loves me better than anyone here on earth can ever love me. I believe that you can always find something good out of something bad. I believe that regardless of where you come from and the poor choices you have made before you got to this very moment in your life, I believe that you can heal from the pain you have had in your life, and you can make a difference in someone else's life. I am reading a wonderful book right now by Max Lucado. He is a Christian author, and he is also a pastor. The book I am reading is called, "Cure for the Common Life."

I just read a chapter about little deeds. The jist of this

chapter is that every kind thing that a person does matters. A little bit of kindness from one person can be a miracle to many.

Maybe writing this book is my little deed. It is painful for me to write my story. I am doing it in hopes that one of you reading this book will need to read my story and that it will make a positive difference in your life. I am praying for you, all of you. For all I know there may only be one person that reads my book. If so, it is worth it for me to do so because maybe something I am sharing will spark hope in you. Maybe it will help you to realize that you can make a difference in whatever it is you do best. Honestly, I don't really know what I do best. I can tell you what has hurt me most and that is what I am writing about. My hope for you is that you use whatever hurts you most and turn bad into good and ugly into beautiful in your life.

I want you to know that if you are reading this book and think that no one cares about you, I am here to tell you that you are wrong. I care and most of all God Cares. Your story is worth telling just as I am beginning to believe that mine is as well. For people like us that have felt as if we never really belonged anywhere and that we don't fit in. You are not alone; you do matter, and you will never be alone. God made you feel different for a reason, he wants you to stand out, he wants you to reach all the millions of people that feel just like you do that can't speak out.

This may sound odd but throughout my life, God has spoken to me through dreams. Many of my dreams are extremely vivid and seem so real that they feel like they are happening in real time.

On 7/29/2009 I had a dream about my mother.
In my dream she was standing in her kitchen weighing almost nothing with a white plastic ring around her waist that was planted on the floor to keep her standing up.
It kind of reminded me of a stand for a Barbie to keep her from falling over. In my dream, my mom was trying to cook dinner, but she looked like she was about to collapse from exhaustion. I picked up my mother and took off the white plastic thing around her waist and held her in my arms like you would a child. I looked directly into her eyes and asked her, "Why couldn't you love me?" She said, "I have always loved you, I never stopped loving you."

In my dream, I continued to carry her around like a precious gem and I longed to speak to her but there were all kinds of people around, so I couldn't. I kept trying to speak to her but for some reason I knew she didn't want to talk to me. I wanted so much to tell her about my life and the life of my children. I wanted to get advice from my mother as I believe most children do. I was starved for the attention I had longed for from her for years. I just wanted her to ask me how I was doing, but she never did.

After I woke up from that dream, I immediately called my brother Tommy. I was crying the entire time I was telling him my dream. I knew in my heart that my mom was close to dying in real life or that she might already be dead.

I made the mistake of calling the same hospital that

I had gone to with my daughter when we were both rejected by my mom.

I found out that she was there in Intensive Care. Apparently, they weren't allowed to give out any information to anyone that called except for Damian and my brother Tommy. At least my mom was still alive which gave me a small ray of hope to one day still be able to see her again.

CHAPTER 22

My Mom's Dying Wish

On September 1st, 2009, I received a call from my brother that would change my life forever. Damian called my brother and told him that he wanted me to call him. He asked my brother to call me and ask if I would phone him. He did not tell my brother what he wanted to speak to me about, but my brother agreed to pass on the message to me. My brother called me, and I could tell something was up because he wasn't joking around with me like he usually did when he called me. He said he had some news for me which usually meant that was news about our mom.

My brother told me that Damian wanted me to call him and that he did not know why. I could tell my brother was worried. He had no idea why Damian wanted me to contact him, and he was concerned about me getting hurt. I agreed to call him and took down the cell phone number that belonged to our father. I felt sick to my stomach, but I called him right away anyway so that I would not chicken out. I called him with a professional business voice that was far from warm. When he said hello, I told him who I was and waited for him to tell me what he wanted. He wanted to see me.

You know that feeling you get when you are going to get sick, and you don't know whether you are going to have diarrhea or if you are going to throw up? This is what I felt like when I heard my father's voice.

He apparently wanted me to meet with him so that he could inform me of my mom's current health state. Why he wanted to meet me in person I still to this day do not know. He wanted to see me that evening or the next morning but couldn't commit to a time. He called me later that evening and left me a message because I missed his call.

He said he wasn't out of his meeting, yet that evening and he didn't know if he would be able to meet that night but that he would phone me back later and let me know.

I returned his call and left him a message. But he never called me back. I mean he NEVER called me back. The next evening, I got a call from my brother telling me that he didn't know what I said to Damian but that I apparently intimidated him so much that he didn't feel comfortable meeting with me anymore. I thought that was extremely ironic considering what he had put me through. I was happy that I didn't have to see him and chalked it up that it wasn't meant to be.

On September 4th I received a call from my brother telling me that my mom was asking for me and wanted me to come see her in the hospital. Of course, I was going to go see her. I had been waiting for years for her to want to see me. However, my brother did not share my joy. He was concerned that she would be mean to me or say unkind things to me that would hurt me, and he told me not to have any expectations of her. I told him that if our mom wanted to say mean things or yell and scream at me it was ok with me. I just wanted to see her again and give her the opportunity to do and say as she wanted with me.

The first time I went to see my mom at the hospital with my daughter, I went to see her for me.
This time, I was going to see her because she asked me to come see her, and she wanted to see me, so I was going to see her for her.
Again, my brother cautioned me, and he asked me an important question. He said, "Faith, what would be the best thing to you that could happen when you saw her? I told him that she would tell me that she is sorry and that she was wrong for what she did, that she would ask God for forgiveness so that she could go to heaven and that she would tell me that she loved me. He then asked what my second favorite thing would be. I said, "that she would tell God she was sorry and ask him for forgiveness."

CHAPTER 23
My Last Visit

I was supposed to call my father (Damian) when I got into the lobby of the hospital my mom was in. I was running late so I called him when I was about 15 minutes away to let him know how much longer I would be. I had stopped off at my favorite flower shop after calling them three times and being unsuccessful in reaching them by phone to order an arrangement for my mother. I didn't want anything big because I knew there wouldn't be space in the hospital room, and I just wanted something small but colorful that would bring a little bit of joy to my mom's situation.

I wanted her to see it and think of me. I wanted it to be simple because I am simple. It ended up being a small round short glass vase that had a few lavender roses and a bunch of different types of flowers and greenery. It was perfect. I got to the hospital and went to the security guy that was sitting at his desk.

I phoned Damian to let him know that I had arrived. My flower arrangement for my mother was in a box to protect it from spilling over in the car ride to the hospital. I went to the security guard and asked if he could help me by throwing away the paper and box that the flower

arrangement was in. He did help me and took away all
that was no longer needed.

I went over to the lobby and stood there waiting for
Damian to come to escort me to the room my mother
was in. No one was allowed to see my mom, so Damian
had to come and escort me upstairs. Of course, those
were his strict instructions and his rules to keep my
mother isolated from everyone.

I saw him long before he saw me. He was now a little old
white-haired man with a small frame. He was looking
around the lobby trying to find me. Was he trying to find
an eighteen-year-old daughter he once knew? Maybe
so, because he did not recognize the forty-two-year-old
woman that was standing right next to him holding
flowers for her mother. I said, "I am right here, I'm Faith." I
would be damned if I called him dad. He never deserved
to be called that. He was shocked that it was me. I could
tell that he was nervous. I wasn't nervous to see him, just
disgusted. I was nervous to see my mom but that was
because I loved her.

He asked me if he could sit down and talk to me a
minute about my mom's situation. I said yes and he sat
down next to me in a chair and told me that my mom
made the decision to stop having her dialysis and some
other treatments that were keeping her alive. He said
that she was too tired and in too much pain to endure
anymore. I could tell that he was trying to manipulate
me by making me sad and feeling sorry for him. It didn't
work. I didn't feel sorry for him, I only felt sorry for my
mom, the one that had endured far too much in her
long life of 70 years.

We went up the elevator and stood outside her room. He asked me to go first, and I said, "No, you go first and make sure she still wants to see me." I was honestly so nervous to see her, and I held my breath as he asked her. He said, "Martha, Faith's here to see you, are you ready to see her? I could hear my mom's voice saying, "Yes."

It has been extremely difficult for me to even think about writing about the last time I saw my mom. I had to go through many years of healing before I even thought about writing it. I am getting very close to finally finishing this book and I realize now that I couldn't write about the last time, I saw my mom because it was one of the main things in my life that still hurts me. I am sure it will hurt me for the remainder of my days, but I know now that God can heal anything because he is healing me. Maybe it takes some of us longer than others to let go of the hurt and embrace the healing. Whatever is hurting you, it can be healed, no matter how big the hurt is. I have learned that God's shoulders are much bigger than ours. He alone has the strength to help us through the darkest of times and bring us into the light.

As I followed Damian through the hospital room door my heart was pounding, I was so scared to see my mom, because I knew in my heart it would be the very last time, I would see her. But, this time, I wasn't going to see her for me, I was there because she wanted to see me. I was ready for her to say whatever she wanted and needed to say to me. I had an extra layer of protection around me because I allowed my invisible walls to go up. I was prepared for my mom to say the worst of the worst to me. The first thing I saw was navy blue soft boot braces on both of my mom's feet and each of her toes bandaged. My mom was so fragile and small. Her eyes were closed, and she looked so broken. I soon found out that she was literally broken. Just about every bone in my mom's body was broken. Every toe was broken, her back was also broken. All her bones were falling apart, all her organs were shutting down and my mom was beyond tired, and she was dying.

Damian told her that I was there, so she tried very hard to open her eyes to no avail. After Damian explained that all her bones were broken and falling apart his phone rang, and it was apparently his alarm company, so he had to go to his house. He asked me if I could stay with my mom until he got back, and I said yes.

I realize now as I am writing this that God had planned for me to spend this time alone with my mom.

After he left the room, I said, "Hi mom, it's me, Faith." She opened her eyes for a brief second trying so hard to keep her eyes open and trying so hard to focus her eyes so she could see me. She said, "I have been so angry with you for so long." Believe it or not, I was angry. I asked her why she had been so angry with me. She told me it was what I said the last time she saw me (She was talking about the confrontation). I proceeded to tell her that I was the child and that I was the victim not Damian (Meanwhile, my mother was going in and out of consciousness). She would try to open her eyes to focus them but gave up trying and with her eyes closed, she said, "No, not that... when you said that I was a terrible mother." (After she said that all I could hear was her crying). She told me that all that time was wasted. I can still hear the way she said w a s t e d....... (It was long and drawn out and you could hear the pain in her voice). *At the time my mother said that to me, I heard her with my ears and head but not until I wrote this did, I truly hear it and feel it with my heart.* (Meanwhile, my mother was going in and out of consciousness), but she still had tears coming out from under her closed eyes.

I found out that day that my mother was holding a grudge against me for all those years because I told her that she failed her job as a mother. She kept calling me Sofia, which is my sister's name. Then I would tell her that I wasn't Sofia, that I was Faith. This happened over and over while we were alone for two and a half hours. I could tell that eventually she felt bad because she would apologize and then call me my sister's name again. I told her that it was ok. I told her she was used to saying my sister's name and that she wasn't used to saying my name for a long time. She would continue to go in and out of consciousness for the remaining time I was with her. She was on heavy pain medication because she was going through such an overwhelmingly huge amount of pain. They had to give her so many strong drugs because if they didn't, she would have probably died from how much pain she was in.

I told her about my daughter and son and what they were doing during that time frame. I told her that they were both beautiful and loving children and the loves of my life.

I had just passed my Real Estate exam a few days before,

so I tried telling her about that. I have no idea how much of it she heard or understood but she tried to open her eyes when I spoke about my children. At that point I realized my mom just wanted to see me to let go of whatever anger she had towards me and in doing so, I think she realized what a waste of time it had all been to hold on to so much anger. I knew then that my mom had regretted how angry she was with me and regretted holding her grudge towards me for so many years.

For any of you reading this book, pay attention to the regret that my mother had for holding such a horrible grudge and for all the wasted years she held anger towards me. It was hurting her for so many years. Imagine the anger and grudge you have been carrying for someone in your life. Let it go.
Life is far too short to hold grudges and keep anger in our hearts.

When we have anger in our hearts it doesn't leave enough room for love.

I remember talking about random things because I didn't know what to say so I asked her about her chili recipe, but as hard as she tried, she couldn't remember it.

Like I said before, this time that I went to the hospital to see my mother, it wasn't for me, I went because she asked for me to come.

As I sat there not knowing what to say to this stranger that was my mom. God put it on my heart that I was on borrowed time being with my mom and since Damian

wasn't there, I needed to take advantage of the time that
we were alone.

God also put the dream I had about her into the
forefront of my mind and I could hear this voice inside
my head telling me to ask her the question, and so I
asked her.

"Mom, why couldn't you love me?" She opened her eyes
and said, "Faith, I have always loved you."

She was all in white, just like in my dream that I had
about her. I know that God gave me the dream so that I
would be prepared to ask her that question that day.

*I cried... the walls that were all around me when I walked
into that hospital room melted away when I realized that
my mom did in fact love me. She was just too sick to fight the
illness and to fight for me.*

Eventually, Damian came back, and the dynamics
changed in that hospital room. He started to manipulate
my mom by telling her how much better she looked
now that she saw me. He proceeded to tell her how she
needed to still do her dialysis and the other procedures
that she had to do 3 to 4 times a week.

In this tiny voice, she said, "No Damian, you know we
already made the decision to stop everything when
we talked with the doctors. I am tired, Damian." He
kept pushing and telling her that he saw the color in
her cheeks, and it must be because she was so happy
that I came to see her. My mother's cheeks were
white as snow.

Even when he saw how miserable and tired my mom

was, he was true to his true nature of being such a selfish and heartless man.

I remember that a nurse brought in my mom's dinner, but my mom had no desire to eat anything. I remember there was some brown mushy stuff that was supposed to be some kind of meat, but I remember it looking like soft dog food. It made me so sad to see my father feeding her that and her making awful faces trying to appease him by choking it down. I remember that he brought her cantaloupe from home and started feeding it to her, which she loved. She told me how Damian did everything for her and that he even washed the dishes (I never saw my father wash a single dish in his entire life!) I could tell this time my mom was trying to manipulate me because she wanted me to make up with him. Fat chance. I just said, "That's nice."

Somehow, my mom and I started talking about chocolate covered cherries which she loved. I told her that the next time I saw her that I would bring her some Godiva dark chocolate covered cherries. I had a tiny false sense of hope that maybe Damian would let me see her again. *To be honest, I know that I knew that this was probably the last time I would get to see her.*

At that point, I knew I needed to leave, but knowing it was the last time made it extremely difficult for me. With tears in my eyes, I kissed my mother on the cheek and told her that I loved her. As I walked out the door of that hospital room, I remember feeling extremely sad but somehow, I knew I had a peace that I didn't have before I went to see my mom that day. I finally had closure with my mom, and I knew that she had closure with me. My mom had made peace with me and the anger that she allowed to control her all those years disappeared.

My mom finally had peace with me.

It did end up being the very last time I ever spoke to my mother; the last time I would hear her voice and the last time I would ever get to see her.

I called Damian so many times asking him if I could see my mom, but he would never allow me to see her again. He told me that the gardener's daughter was with her at the hospital. I have no idea why he told me that, but I am sure it was to hurt me. I guess it was supposed to mean that she would rather spend time with his gardener's daughter than with her own daughter.

Whatever the reason, it did hurt me. I finally stopped calling him because I could tell that he enjoyed having the power to keep her from me once again. I was having difficulty functioning every day because I was already in mourning from not being able to see my mom and I knew for my own well being I finally had to let go, and I did.

I am grateful that we both experienced healing that day. I still don't understand why the promise I thought God made me of reuniting me and my children with my mom didn't come true, but I now receive the fact that I got to spend over two hours alone with my mom 3 weeks before she died,

and I heard with my own ears my mom tell me that she
always loved me.

Sometimes we believe for so long that certain things will
happen in our lives and when they don't happen as we
had dreamed, they would happen we become extremely
devastated by the disappointment. As you probably guessed,
this happened to me.

I want you to know that I lost my faith for a whole year
after my mom died. I was very angry with God for not
keeping the promise that I believed with all my heart that he
made to me.

I was in a deep depression like I had never known before.
Trust me when I say, I have been extremely depressed many
times in my life.

I was so filled with grief by the loss of my mom and the hope
that she would ever have relationships with my children and
me that I couldn't see the gift of time and healing that God
did give me.

My kids never knew my mom, my mom never knew my kids.
For that matter, my mom never really knew me. For that, I
will always hold sadness in my heart.

I realize that we all have free will to act on things in life how
we feel at the time is right. However, there are consequences
to our actions and our choices in our lives.

For my mom, she didn't know my children or me. She
would eventually end up being without all her children and
grandchildren because of her husband.

Don't let time pass without trying to heal the broken
relationships that you value in your life. Life is too short to
waste time. I picture my mom saying:

"All that time W A S T E D!" I can still hear the desperation in her crying while she said it. That is exactly what it was, it was wasted time.

Reach out to that person or people in your life that you need healing with and remember that God can heal anything and anyone, even a wretch like me.

CHAPTER 24

My Mom's Last Day

I remember it was a Friday when my brother Tommy, had gone to see my mom to say his last goodbye's. The doctor's had taken my mom off all the treatments they were doing for her on the day before and sent her home to die in the comfort of her own home.

I had purchased a small four count box of Godiva dark chocolate covered cherries for my brother to give to my mom along with a personal card that I wrote to her. Since my father would not allow me to see my mom, my brother Tommy read the card aloud to her on my behalf.

My brother Tommy told me that our mom could no longer speak or open her eyes. He also told me that she no longer had tears to cry but that he could tell she was crying as he read aloud the card that I wrote her. My brother told her that I had sent her the Godiva Chocolates as well.
My brother later told me that he cried the whole time he was reading my card to her.

I left my son at home while I went to pick up my daughter from work. I only got about three minutes away and I realized that I had to get as close to my mom as possible. I had a sense of urgency that I could not overlook. I called my son, Declan and told him to be ready when I got home. He asked me where we were going, and I told him that we were going to drive to my mom's house and park at the end of the street so that I could be as close to her before she died.

I picked up my daughter Sierra and told her where we were going and then we picked up my son. The whole way to my mom's house I was filled with sadness because I knew it would be the last time I would ever go there when she would still be alive in the house, I grew up in. I was right.

I remember that it was already dark outside as we parked at the bottom of the cul de sac and we just looked at the house. I was explaining to my son which rooms had lights on and where my mom was in the house.

Apparently, they had a bed downstairs in the playroom by the pool table, just behind the garage doors that we could see from the street. *In my mind I can still see us sitting there now with such a huge desire to go inside so I could take one more last glimpse of my mother before she left this world.*

When I got home, I went to bed and cried. I had a chat with my grandpa who passed away six years before on September 27th. I told him that my mom was dying that night and to please be ready for her. I asked him to bring all the other dead friends and relatives that loved my mother so that she wouldn't be alone. I don't remember falling asleep, but I know that I did because when the phone rang at 1:41 am on September 26th, I knew my mom had passed on. I looked at the phone and it was the front gate to where I lived. I opened the gate and said out loud to myself, "She is dead, my mom is dead." I ran downstairs and opened the door like a crazy woman. My brother came up to the door and we both hugged one another and cried. I realized at that moment that I wasn't invited to the funeral. I told my brother that and he said, "You are going to the funeral, we are both going." We decided to invite the people closest to us so that we were surrounded by love as we faced the most painful thing either of us ever experienced before this moment in both of our lives. We decided that we would have our own reception afterward in my home. *I am crying now. I guess I couldn't write before now because I knew it would hurt too much. Today is October 11th, 2009. It has only been 15 days since my mom left this world.*

A lot has happened since my mom died.

The morning that my mom died, when I was walking my dog, and no one was outside. I looked up at the blue sky wondering how it could be blue and how the world didn't end because my mom was gone.

As I was walking my dog feeling like God had forgotten about me and trying so hard not to let the tears escape my eyes. I noticed a car passing by me and realized it was one of my neighbors driving by. I had no idea who was driving the car that day but what I can tell you is all I saw was their daughter Cloe who was four years old at the time. The minute Cloe saw me, a huge smile appeared on her precious face. She was smiling at me from the back seat of the car, and she was waving to me. She had no idea that I had just found out about five hours before that my mother had just died. I can tell you that God planted that beautiful little girl in my life that day, to remind me that he hadn't forgotten about me. It's amazing the power of the simple act of a smile, especially coming from a small child.

The Circle of Life popped into my mind. My therapist Sharon called me a few days before my mom died, she told me her second grandchild was going to be born on Wednesday, September 30th, 2009, it ended up being the same day of my mom's funeral.

I knew my mom was in a far better place than this one. She wasn't in pain anymore both physically and mentally. She was at peace now.
My mom had given up her own family along with me. Why? Because I believe that she only had one fight left in her and that was to try to fight her disease. Do I think she chose the right fight? No, but it wasn't a decision that was mine to make. My mom was very different from me, from her sisters and from her own mom. She was very naive. She was a wife that believed that you stand by your husband no matter what. She was never happy unless she was around those that she loved. It has been so long since I can remember ever seeing her happy or smiling for that matter. She was never free to be happy around Damian. He was too insecure for that. He wanted to be the only one or thing in her life. In the end, he got exactly what he wanted. He removed all her children, all

her grandchildren, her sisters, her brothers, her friends and even her mom. My mother died a loving wife. Not a loving mother, not a loving grandmother, not a loving daughter, not a loving sister or a loving friend like she once was but only a loving wife because that was the consequence to the road that she chose. My mother died on September 26th, 2009, at about 12:30am.
My brother got a phone call from one of the nuns in the Catholic church that was in the house my mom died in at the time of her death, along with a 24-hour nurse that was at my mom's side. I wish I could have been the one at her side (Instead I was parked on the street with my children in the car crying). If I was able to be near her, I would have never left her side until the Lord came to take her. In my heart I know that somehow, she knows that now, even though she probably doubted that all these years. How sad that she never allowed me to love her the way she deserved to be loved and she never allowed herself to love me or any of the people that she cared for the way God intended her to love.

God gives us all free will and we need to decide between good and evil and right and wrong. We need to pay the consequences for the poor decision making that we make. We are guilty of making bad decisions even when we aren't aware they are bad. Unfortunately, for those of us who loved my mom, not only did we have to suffer the loneliness without her but also had to see for ourselves that in the end, my mom was far lonelier than we were.

On her coffin, there were only two words written on a peach-colored ribbon that draped over the wooden box:

"Loving Wife."

Yes, she was a loving wife. She proved that all the years that she stood by her husband's side after knowing that he physically, mentally, and sexually abused her daughter. In the end, I realize that my mom was abused by him as well and in so many ways. The mental hold he had on her was extremely strong for her to let go of her motherly instincts.

Now she is in peace and the peace I have is knowing that she finally got away from him because he cannot follow her where she is going.

THE DAY BEFORE MY MOM'S FUNERAL

Honestly, there is very little that stands out in my mind about the day before my mom's funeral. However, what I do remember is very profound and meaningful to me. I guess I have to say that I was numb, my heart was numb, and I was here but not here.

I remember two of my good friends; Daisy and Carolyn came over to my house, honestly, I couldn't tell you why or how they even knew to come over because that was like a blur.

My friend Carolyn brought her young daughter Alexa with her. (I think Alexa was about seven years old). She ran up to me and in front of my daughter and my two friends she hugged me hard and said, "I am sorry your mommy died." I lost it. I hung on to Alexa and cried my eyes out, along with my two friends and my daughter. It's amazing the kind of power that a child's love can give when it is needed most.

CHAPTER 25
My Mother's Funeral

My brother dropped off some ice chests and some stuff for the reception the night before the funeral and he was leaving to go pick up my niece from the airport and bring her back to my house (My niece lives in a different state).

My daughter and my niece drove with me to the church on the morning of my mother's funeral. On the way to the church, I stopped at Starbucks because my stomach was really upset and I needed to use the restroom. *Every time I pass that Starbucks, I think of the day my mom was buried in the ground, it's a good thing I am seldom in that area.*

We got to the church and my brother was already there and so was my cousin's wife on my mom's side. I was so uncomfortable, nervous, and scared. You see, I wasn't invited to my mother's funeral. No one on my mom's side of the family was invited or welcomed to come, least of all, me.

I later found out that my father told everyone that I was not allowed to come. Funny how things don't make sense. Wasn't I the one who was treated badly, wasn't I the child that was taken advantage of by the manipulating father? Even after my mother's death he continued to hate me when I never wronged him.

I realize now, so many years later that the sight of me must have reminded him each time he saw me of his terrible actions.

All I am, was a reminder of his horrible actions and behavior.

Maybe he needed to hate me so that he could live with himself. My brother was a pallbearer. My father was waiting for him and shortly after we arrived, he came outside to come and get him. He looked at me with disgust and hatred and never said one word to me. I never said one word to him either. I had nothing left to say or do for this man.

My mother was dead and any obligation to be decent to him, died when my mother died. I no longer had to be polite to him or treat him like anything other than what he was. In my mind, in my heart and in my soul, this man was NOT my father. He was merely the tool to get me here into this world. *I use the word tool in both senses of the word.*

My mother always wanted a closed casket. Ever since I was a little girl, and we went to funerals she would remind me that she wanted a closed casket and that she couldn't understand how anyone would want an open casket. She would say, "I don't want people looking at me when I am dead." *I can hear her saying that and I must admit that it made me smile.*

She reminded me quite often because she was often on her deathbed.

At some point my daughter Sierra, who was holding my

hand for most of the day, walked me into the church. All
my father's family was there including my father. I saw
my brother off to the side with my father just closing
the casket. (I guess my father had opened the coffin for
a moment for my brother to see my mom.) I motioned
to my brother that I wanted to see her, so my daughter
and I squeezed through all the people to get to the other
side where my brother, my father and the coffin were.
My daughter had a death grip on my hand as to reassure
me that she was my protector, and she was.
We made it to the other side and my brother told my
father that I wanted to see my mom. My father told him
that we weren't allowed to open the coffin anymore
He lied... The lady in charge of the service overheard
my father tell my brother that and said that it was no
problem to open it.

My brother was stern with my father and told him again
in a very firm voice that I wanted to see our mom. He
said, "Fine, but only for a minute."

They opened the coffin...she was wearing a light mint
green matching outfit. Her eyes were closed, her hands
were crossed upon her chest (the way I had seen her
sleep a million times when she was taking her naps). I
almost didn't have enough time to see her hands, her
fingers looked just like mine. I had to see her hands even
if for only a moment. Damian (my father) closed the
coffin only a few seconds after it had been opened.
My knees buckled and I could feel my daughter and my
brother holding me.

They walked me into the right side of the church where I realized I was crying uncontrollably.

My brother had to leave to go get ready to be one of the pallbearers, so it was up to my 16-year-old daughter to help me regain control of my emotions. I remember she took me over to where there were candles lit and I crouched down in the corner on the floor crying like a baby. I refused to get up or move until I heard a voice of someone else telling me how much my mom loved me. I didn't look up, I only said through my sobs, "How do you know that?" I didn't even look up because I muttered it in between my sobs. She said, "Because your mom told me." I turned around and looked up and saw this short little old nun that said she was with my mom when she died and that my mom told her how happy she was to spend time with me 3 weeks prior to her death. I got up, wiped my tears, blew my nose, and put on my sunglasses when I had finally turned around, the nun was gone.

My daughter and I saw my friends and support group and we found a seat in the back left side of the church. Some of my close friends and even one of my neighbors that I didn't even know very well came to support me. They never even met my mom, nor did they know the whole situation.

The church they had the service at was at a different church than the one we grew up going to. Thankfully, the service was long. I wanted it to be long. I wanted that moment to last as long as possible. As long as the service kept going, it didn't have to end. At one point, I got up and went to the bathroom and went to look at the pictures that were in the lobby of the church. All the pictures were either of my mom alone or with Damian. No friends, no family, no kids, no grandkids, no relatives of any kind. It was creepy. I was about to steal an 8 ½ x 11 senior high school photo of my mom but about 5 of my friends came out after me. They were worried about me and thought that I was outside crying. Right behind them was the lady in charge so I had to abandon my idea of stealing the photograph of my mom and went back to my pew in the back.

The only one to give a eulogy was my mom's cousin. He was the only relative on my mom's side that was invited. Apparently, he wasn't allowed to mention that my mom had any kids, grandkids, a mother, sisters, brothers, or uncles. I think he mentioned once something about my grandfather that had died. All he talked about was how great Damian was and what a great wife my mom was. Honestly, it was a bunch of crap. As I mentioned before, the ribbon on the coffin read: Loving Wife.
There was no mention of her ever conceiving a child. How sad, even in death he controlled her. It didn't matter to her anymore, she was free.

CHAPTER 26
Blessings of Love

When I got to the cemetery where they were going to bury my mom, I saw two familiar faces that I was very happy to see...

One of my mom's best friends that lived around the corner from her house was standing next to the grave site with her daughter Mila. I had known their family since I was a little girl. Her family was one of the only other hispanic families that lived in our neighborhood growing up that I knew, and her family was like family to our family. We knew their entire family growing up because we went to all the parties and get-togethers that they had, and they knew all our family because they came to all the parties we had.

I had always wished that Elizabeth was my mom, and that Mila was my little sister. I always loved both like they were immediate family. I ran up to them and hugged Mila and teased her by calling her Pinky (Her dad always called her pinky as a nickname out of love because she loved pink and growing up, I always teased her about it. Her dad would ask me," Are you jealous?" I would tell him, "Yes, of course I am"). I remember Mila was holding

her 9-month-old beautiful baby girl named Sienna when I saw her for the first time.
Next, I hugged Elizabeth, I can't tell you how happy I was to see them.

I had gone to Elizabeth's door two different times throughout the years, but she wasn't home either time. I know now that it was probably best that she wasn't home when I went by her house because I realize now that my mom needed her far more than I did and if Elizabeth ever knew about what happened to me it would have been too difficult for her to be around my father and not say something about it.

At other times in this book, I have told you how God always puts people in our lives to fill the holes that are left in us when loved ones pass on from this world and physically leave us.
As you now know, the loss of my mom was a truly devastating loss to me. The day of my mom's funeral, God put people that I had always loved back into my life and even more people for me to love and to love me back.
It is so difficult for me to put into words the unconditional love that I feel for the old friends that have become family to me, my kids, and my husband.
All of them became my extended family. God healed the huge holes that I had in my heart where the loss of my mom lived. He filled it with each one of them.
I have been blessed with more family for me and my kids.
I now have a mom, another sister, another brother,

and more nieces and nephews that I have a very close bond with.

I have spent the past 14 years celebrating birthdays and holidays, celebrations of life, victories and milestones and also sharing tears, heartache and loss.

It's funny how God puts certain people in our lives when we need them most, even at a cemetery...

God's timing is perfect. When I was at the end of my rope and as low as I think I have ever been in my life, God sent me blessings of love.

Some people only stay for a season in our lives and some you are blessed to have for your entire lives. I am forever grateful that God put these special people back into my life and in doing so, the pool of people that I love has grown even bigger.

my grandma

My grandmother on my mom's side was one of the first people whom I knew really loved me and that didn't want anything in return. My mom's biological mother passed away when my mom was nine months old. Some say she died from pneumonia and others said it was because of complications in childbirth. My grandma became my mom's mother when my mother was 2 ½ years old. I found this out one day when I was a little girl. I remember my two older brothers and I were watching a small black and white TV in my parents' bedroom and my mom came in, turned off the TV and announced that my grandma was not my REAL grandma. I proceeded to call my mother a liar and got slapped on the face for talking back. I cried and cried when she told us. I was really way too young to understand what that meant besides the fact that grandma was not my grandma (But she was my grandma whether she had physically given birth to my mother or not. She raised my mother as her own since my mom was 2 1/2 years old. She was the only mom that my mother ever knew). My mother probably had no idea how to tell us so she just told us not knowing how hurt and upset we would be. You see, grandma was the love of my life. She always had been since I could remember. She was an amazing and loving woman that loved me with no strings attached. Unconditional love comes to mind because that is how well she loved me.

I found a birthday card with a $20 bill still taped on the left-hand side of the card. *I couldn't bear the thought of ever removing the money because my grandma's hands are the ones that strategically taped the money onto the card.* Lots of love and care went into getting the tape and taping it there in that exact spot. Those are the soft wrinkled hands that brushed my hair a thousand times when I was a little girl and a young woman.

I realize how very blessed I was to be loved so well. A heart that hurts after a loved one passes on is a heart that truly loved and was loved well.

I have learned throughout my life that it doesn't matter if someone is blood related or not. To me the importance of family isn't defined by having the same blood line. God puts people in our lives when we need them and oftentimes, they aren't blood relatives but start out as good friends and over time become like family. Sometimes they just start out as family. I am so blessed to know this firsthand because there are special family members in my life that are not blood related, including my grandma.

If there has ever been that person in your life that you know that you knew with all your being that they would always love you, no matter where they are, no matter where you are, no matter how long it had been since you had last spoken to them.

A person in this world that would love you and not judge you no matter what and believed in you far more than you ever felt you could believe in yourself. If you have a special person like this that is still alive today, then tell them in the best way you know how to tell them how very important they are to you and who they are to you in this life. Life goes by so quickly and oftentimes we get too busy in this life to share positive thoughts and meaningful words to those that are special to us.

That special someone has always been and will always be, my beautiful grandma that just passed away on May 21st, 2013. My grandma was such an important part of my life, of my being and the ultimate love I have and will ever know.

I told her things I would be ashamed to ever tell another soul. My grandma used to tell me that she would never tell anyone anything I told her unless I wanted her to. She used to say that she would take all my secrets to her grave and recently, she did. When we were at the cemetery and we all lined up to put dirt on her grave, I kept thinking about how my beloved grandma took all my secrets to her grave and I could not stop crying no matter how hard I tried. I used to tell her when I was a little girl that I was going to die first because I could never stand to be in this world without her here with me. She was my biggest fan, and she was the greatest cheerleader in my life. She used to tell me that she was going to die first because she was older, and she couldn't stand to be without me. We used to tease one another all the time about who loved each other more. I would say I loved her more because I was younger and had more energy to love her more. She would tell me she loved me more because she was older and had loved me even longer than I could remember. She used to tell me that she fell in love with me the first moment she laid her eyes on me. She said I was a very chubby baby and when she first saw me, I was wrapped up in a blanket and the moment she saw my face she fell completely in love with me. My grandma was my best friend. I told her everything. We talked about sex; we talked about love. We talked about everything you can possibly think about. We loved watching old movies, we loved going to the movies and eating popcorn with Milk Duds. It was grandma's favorite and she taught me to eat popcorn with Milk Duds too.

I wish I could remember the last movie we saw together. I guess it doesn't really matter. The truth of it is, grandma never remembered the names of the movies we saw and when my grandpa was alive, he couldn't remember either. We all just loved going to the movies together and we also loved staying home and watching old black and white movies. One time when my grandfather was still alive, I took my grandma to go see a Jim Carey movie that I didn't do any research on. The movie was called Me, Myself and Irene. The movie was rated R and there was a boy that looked to be about eight years old in the movie theater that sat right next to my grandma. The movie was not appropriate for the eight-year-old boy, my grandma or even me. The funny thing is, the only name of any movie both of my grandparents could ever remember was: Me, Myself and Irene and of course they told the whole family about it. They both teased me mercilessly until the day each one of them died. To say the least it was the most uncomfortable I ever felt in a movie theater. Thinking back, I have no idea why we didn't leave. My grandma kept looking at the little boy and back to the screen which showed exposed breasts and foul language and back to the little boy again and the look of disgust was clearly on her face. I have to say, I never felt so embarrassed. It made a great joke for the remaining 13 years of my grandma's life.

That reminds me how God always turns something bad into something good. We had a lot of laughs because of that movie, they just all happened for the 13 years after we saw it.

I started making up poems before I could even write. I think it was one way of expressing so many feelings I had inside. My grandmother always encouraged my writing and was constantly telling me how talented I was. I remember her always getting upset at the thought of my parents because they would always shut me up and not listen to me. I was an invisible child that could not be heard nor seen until it was of benefit to either of my parents. My grandma noticed that and despised them for treating me that way. When I was in my early 20's I would go over to my grandparent's house and I would tell my grandma whatever unhappiness I was going through at the time and she would sit me on her couch, get a brush and gently brush my hair for hours until it felt like silk (My hair was always long). I would cry and cry and she would brush and brush. She would share with me things that made her sad. The two of us would cry for each other and we would continue to grow closer throughout the years. I have since told my grandmother all my shortcomings and all the mistakes that I have made in my life and still she did not judge me. She knew everything there was to know about me and still my grandma loved me anyway. For the entirety of my life, my grandma has consistently told me how much she loved me and has always shown me.

One morning after my grandpa died, I took her to breakfast at Carrows and we were discussing how much we missed my grandpa, and I was telling her how I keep running into situations where I know grandpa is there with me. I asked her, "Grandma, if you die before I do, how will I know if you are with me?" Her reply was merely, "You will know." I said, "But how will I know?" "You'll hear me say, "I love you."

The funny thing is that she has always told me that she loves me since I was a little girl (Really since I was born). Although yesterday was the 10-year anniversary of her death, my grandma was right, I can still hear her telling me, "I love you."

The thing is, when we love someone as much as I loved my grandma, all the memories we shared together stay with us forever. I can hear my grandma's voice cheering me on and loving me from Heaven.

I got remarried in April of 2013 after being a single mom for 11 ½ years. My grandma died at the age of 94 a little over a month after my wedding. I was devastated. Right after she died, I needed her so desperately because my marriage was extremely difficult, and I felt so lost and alone. When I remarried it was a huge adjustment for everyone involved.

I wanted, no, I needed so badly to drive to my grandma's house and just have her hold me in her arms and tell me that everything would be ok. You could say I was having a melt down. I was crying and praying. I was asking God to please tell my grandma that I wasn't ok and that I needed her. I just started talking to my grandma out loud while crying. I kept on saying, "Grandma, I am not okay, I need you."

The next day I received a text from My Aunt Becky, who was my mom's youngest brother's wife. That was the day that my grandma sent me reinforcements in my life...

CHAPTER 28
Aunt Becky's Dream

The next morning, I woke up with swollen eyes, nose, and face from crying so much the day before.

I received a text from my Aunt Becky (My mom's youngest brother's wife). Ever since I sent the letter to my mom's side of the family, I started developing a closer relationship with my Aunt Becky but nothing like the relationship that I have developed with her today because of my grandma.

I remember that day, On June 26, 2013, I received this text from my Aunt Becky:

Good morning, I am at work but wanted to tell you I had a dream about grandma last night, it felt so real! In the dream she asked about you and seemed very concerned.
Are you okay?

My response: *Not really...how weird! I have been talking out loud to grandma the last couple of days and telling her how unhappy I am.*

My aunt called me, and she told me her dream...

My grandma and my aunt were in the extra bedroom lying in the bed. My Aunt Becky was so happy to be with my grandma. She said she felt so warm and comfy. She said it felt so comforting to be laying there with my grandma. She said they were just talking but she couldn't remember what about when suddenly, my grandma turned towards her and told her, "Faith is not okay." My aunt told her, "No mom, she is okay." My grandma kept saying, "No, she is not okay!" She apparently said it many times, so many times that when my aunt woke up, she was worried about me, and it prompted her to contact me.

Again, the power of prayer is stronger than many may think.

The power of my grandma's love, even beyond the grave, is still just as powerful as it was when she was here with me on earth. I believe that my grandma sent my aunt to me so that my aunt and I had an even stronger bond then we already had. I believe that my grandma knew that we both needed her so much that she gave us each other.

I truly believe that when a loved one is taken away from us, God puts other significant people in our lives to fill the holes in our hearts where the emptiness of loss dwells within us.

God is truly the only one that can fill up the holes that we have that live inside us. When we embrace him and the love that he has for us, we can learn to embrace the people that he sends for us to love and embrace the love that they have for us in our lives.

CHAPTER 29

Phone Call From Uncle Lewis

One day in the beginning of April 2015 I received a phone call from my Uncle Lewis (My father's youngest brother). He caught me off guard when he called me because I didn't even know that he had my phone number.
He told me that my father was in an induced coma. Apparently, he had gone to Mexico and gotten so sick that he ended up catching pneumonia. He was so ill that the doctors put him in an induced coma thinking that he would get better. However, they could not take him out of the coma.
He was dying now so my uncle contacted each one of my siblings and I because he felt it was the right thing to do.
Although, my siblings and I hadn't spoken to my father for many years. My uncle was trying to urge me to go see my father, but I told him that I had no desire to see him, so I thanked him for letting me know but I didn't want to see my father. My uncle asked me to come to his house to meet a nun that was with my mom when she died. Apparently, the nun wanted to see me. I did end up

going with my husband to see my uncle and the nun he wanted us to meet.

I think it might have been the same nun that spoke to me at the church at the funeral of my mom but to be honest, I am not sure because I never saw the nun at the church, I only caught a glimpse of her, and I only heard her voice when I was devastated and full of despair.

The nun wanted to speak to me alone, so my husband sat and talked with my uncle whom he had never even met before. The Nun told me that I should go see my father in the hospital because it was the right thing to do, but I told her that if she knew what I knew then she wouldn't think so. She said that she did know what I knew. I told her that I had no interest in ever seeing him again. What else she spoke to me about I couldn't tell you because for some reason my mind has blocked it out. I tend to do that when things are extremely difficult for me. I had only gone to my uncle's house to meet her for my uncle's sake.

We didn't stay very long at his house and when we left, I was upset, angry and had a lot of other bad feelings that I can no longer describe. However, I did think about seeing him so that I could forgive him and let go of all the anger that had built up inside of me.

My uncle called me the next day urging me to go see my father. When I got off the phone with my uncle, my sister that I hadn't seen or heard from for six years, (the last time I saw her was the day after my mom's funeral when I drove her back to Vegas) called me and wanted to come stay at my house so she could go see my father

at the hospital. After talking with my sister and praying about it, I decided that I would go see my father with my sister.
She did come to my house and stay for a few days, and we did go to the hospital to see our father.

My sister and I called our brother who lived in Pennsylvania who was disabled and unable to travel. We had him on the phone so that he could say whatever he needed to say to our father who was in a coma who could hear but could not open his eyes and could not speak or move. Damian was also paralyzed. I told him who I was and that I had come to tell him that I forgave him. I have no idea what my sister said but I know that after I spoke to my father, my brother said that he also forgave him. We left the hospital and I felt lighter than I had before I went into his room. I finally let go. We went back to the hospital one or two more times because my sister wanted to go see our father, so I went with her and each time I told him that I forgave him.

It was so ironic to me that my father couldn't speak, he could no longer verbally abuse me. My father could no longer move, he could no longer physically or sexually abuse me. He could no longer see me, and I never wanted him to see me again. He had no choice but to keep his thoughts to himself. He was not able to say or do anything and I was free to forgive him without his selfish ways interrupting me. The way he left this world was so appropriate. *God is so good.*
I never fully understood forgiveness until I truly forgave my father. I have learned that forgiveness isn't really for the

person that we are forgiving but for ourselves. You see, when we hold grudges and anger towards a person, they are not the ones suffering, we are. I had been carrying so much hurt, so much pain and anger that it was hard for me to live my life because I couldn't move forward in living my life because I was hurting myself more by hanging on to all the pain I had carried for so long. Let go of your pain, your hurt, your anger, it wasn't meant for you to carry those things. Forgive those that have wronged you because who are we not to forgive someone no matter how awful they may have hurt you. Think of all the people you may have hurt over the years, whether it was intentional or unintentional.

How can God ever forgive us if we aren't willing to forgive those that have hurt us?

CHAPTER 30

My Father's Funeral

Can you believe there was none?

My father planned everything the way he always did. Precise, calculated and always with an ulterior motive. Even in death. My father made sure that none of us kids would have the convenience of being in a group setting with his side of the family. He didn't want to give us the opportunity of revealing his horrible secrets. So instead of having a funeral he had instructions for his body to be sent straight to the cemetery after his body was ready for burial.

We had no idea when he would be buried, we only knew where because he already shared the same headstone as our mother. My sister and one of my brother's had a desire to know when he was buried, along with my father's brother's and sister's. Since I was the one who lived the closest to the cemetery, I felt that it was up to me to find out any information that I could.

So, after my father died, I took a field trip to the cemetery to try and get some information for everyone who wanted to know. Unfortunately, I couldn't find any. I called my father's youngest brother, Uncle Lewis, and told him I couldn't find any information. You see, my mother's cousin Rufus cut off all my aunts and uncles except for my Aunt Hortencia. None of my father's brothers and sisters knew when he would be buried or when the funeral was. My Uncle Lewis was the one that called each of my siblings and I to inform us of when my father was dying, so he was immediately cut off from visiting my father in the hospital and from knowing the status of my father's health. Cousin Rufus changed his phone number because he got so many calls from my father's family inquiring about his health.

I went back to the cemetery the very next day and saw my mothers grave roped off. I knew my father would be buried soon (I called my Uncle Lewis to let him know).

I saw a truck and some men on the other side of the cemetery, so I followed them in my car. I pulled the driver over and asked him what day a person would be buried if the grave was roped off? He said, "The next day." This was a Tuesday that I was at the cemetery.

I immediately called my Uncle Lewis and told him, so he got a hold of everyone who wanted to go and was able to attend the burial and they all showed up the next day (I personally had no desire to attend).

Unfortunately, it was the wrong day. However, they found out the burial was scheduled for the next day, Thursday morning. Again, I did not go, nor did any of my brother's or my sister. Damian didn't want us there and I personally had no desire to attend the burial of a man I did not respect or even like, even if he was my father. In the end, my father got what he wanted as he usually did.

Only my Aunt Hortencia and her daughter were invited

to attend. My Uncle Lewis said they were shocked to see the family there. You see, my Aunt Hortencia was the only member of the family that knew about Damian's health and was the only one being informed about everything. She wasn't taking any calls from her family either and not sharing any information with them. Cousin Rufus was as far away as he could possibly be from the burial site but close enough to see everyone that was in attendance. He was with his wife, alone watching from a long distance away. He didn't come down the hill. My uncle said he was driving my fathers new Porsche. He would not face any of the family that he had been avoiding for months. The same day they buried my father in the ground (April 16, 2015) I received a call from my husband (he was out of town on business) he said he was flying home and we needed to drive to a city about 2 ½ hours away as soon as he got home from the airport because his mom was just admitted into the hospital (This was the same day my father was buried). She ended up dying early Saturday morning (April 18th, 2015).

It is strange how easy and quick death comes to those around us when we least expect it. That is why we need to try to make peace with the people that have hurt us in this life and ask for forgiveness from those that we have hurt.

My father created so much dysfunction in our household that each of us was filled with our own dysfunction and major core issues. He cultivated anger and guilt within each one of us. None of us were ever good enough to him, even our own mother who stood by his side through all the horrible things he did to all of us.

It was extremely difficult for me to receive that first call from my Uncle Lewis telling me my father was in a coma and that I needed to go say goodbye. I didn't want anything to do with my father and never wanted to see him again.

However, I realize what a huge gift it was for me to have the opportunity to choose to go to see my father and allow myself to forgive him. Forgiving him helped me heal myself. When I received the call that my father died, I remember crying to my husband and telling him that I was so worried that my father was going to hell. I felt very sorry for my father and cried a lot of tears for him. I think this was also a sign of the forgiveness that I had given my father.

I pray that each one of you that needs to forgive someone in your life experiences the same kind of healing that I was blessed to receive. I realize that this is not an easy task, but I believe that you are brave, and that God will give you the inner strength that you need to let go of your anger and allow peace to reign in your heart.

CHAPTER 31

The Estate Sale

One day not long after my father passed away, I received a call from Elizabeth (one of my mom's best friends that I had known since I was a child) telling me that a neighbor had called her to tell her that there was an estate sale happening at my parent's house.
To be honest, I was overcome with deep sadness.
I pictured my childhood home with all my parent's material belongings and none of our family to be a part of such a sad occasion. Sadder still was the fact that they chose this outcome by the choices they had made in their lives.

Life is so short and the choices that we make in this life will impact the lives of our children and grandchildren, and their children and their grandchildren. I urge you to be aware of the decisions that you are making in your life, both small and big. Your choices can hurt or help and heal others.
The choice is entirely yours, seek God for guidance.
He is the only certainty in this world.

Elizabeth immediately called me and started walking over to their house. She asked me if I wanted to go, and I told her that I did not. However, the desire to see the house that I grew up in and the chance to say goodbye to my mom who died in that house (even though I knew she wasn't there anymore) put a heaviness on my heart that I can't explain. I didn't want any material things from them. What I wanted was something neither of them could ever give me. All I ever wanted from them was the love of a good mother and father.

When Elizabeth got to their house, one of the neighbors' sons who I went to school with when I was young, had a few of our family photo albums. He told Elizabeth that there were more photo albums and there was a poem I had written when I was young on a white canvas in one of the upstairs bedrooms. Elizabeth ended up buying that poem from the estate sale along with 3 family photo albums that I later gave to my sister. I found out that Damian had thrown away all the photos of me after my mom died.

This is what the poem said that I wrote:

God

Sometimes when I feel sad and lonely.

I'll say a prayer or two and eventually "God" will send me an answer and tell me just what to do.

I tell him how I'm feeling and ask him why it has to be, then he smiles and says, "My child, your life is like branches on a tree."

He doesn't talk to me out loud, yet I hear him very clear, instead he tells me within myself and with every shedded tear. It's hard to explain to someone who doesn't believe in him as I do. He's just a feeling and faith I have and if you want to bad enough you can believe in him too.

Sometimes when I'm happy I'll call upon my friend and thank him for always being with me and loving me to the end. You feel him in your heart, and you hear him there too. He's such a wonderful feeling, and he's inside of me and you.

Written By: Faith

I need to tell you that after typing the poem I wrote when I was young, I was overcome with great sadness for the little lonely girl who wrote it. I must admit that it is the first time that I understand how important it is for us to grieve and comfort ourselves for the deep hurts that were put upon us as children. I remember early on in one of my therapy appointments with my therapist. I was asked to close my eyes and pretend that I walked into a room where a little girl was crying (The little girl was supposed to be me when I was little) but she wanted me to go into that room and comfort her as the grown adult that I was at the time.

I couldn't do it. I honestly wouldn't and couldn't do it at the time. I realize at this very moment that I just did it when I read my own poem that I wrote so many years ago. To be honest, I almost didn't include the poem because it was in storage somewhere where I hid it from myself because I wasn't brave enough to read it at the time Elizabeth gave it to me. Yesterday, I had this huge urge to go find it, so I went to my storage unit and when I opened the storage door, it was *the first thing that I saw. God has a special way of nudging us out of our stubborn and defiant moments when he has a plan for us. Sadness for my younger self was not the only feeling I had, nor the only lesson that I learned. It was a reminder to me just how long God has been in my life and how he has never left me. My heart is filled with so much gratitude to God for always being at my side even in the most painful and loneliest moments of my life. I realize now that I had to go through all of the pain and struggles, I went through to grow into the woman God wanted me to be, a woman that is open to God using her for his glory.*

When Elizabeth went into the house, I remember her telling me how eerie it was. She said that my parents' whole entire house and all their belongings were still intact. Each drawer had all the stuff it always had in them, every cupboard, every drawer and even my parents' clothes were hanging in the closets. Elizabeth said she was so sad seeing all these people in my mom's house grabbing stuff to buy.

It was sad for her because she loved my mom, she was her friend. It made me very sad to think about how my parents lived their lives. They chose not to have relationships with their own children, they chose to live their lives like they never had children when they did in fact have four.

I would be devastated for my home to be left to strangers going through all my personal belongings, rummaging through to get good buys. My mom would be so sad to have all those strangers going through all her things.

Although my mom chose to stay her whole life with such an awful husband who verbally abused her, who constantly put her down and physically beat her when she was already so ill. I felt so sorry for her, everything that was left of her was just stuff in a house. She couldn't pass down the things that had meaning to her to her children. That was the consequence of staying with an abusive husband that was jealous of any affection or love she gave to any of her kids. She learned very quickly not to give too much affection and eventually it hardened her heart.

In life, we have choices to make. All the decisions that we make have consequences. Some good and some bad. I believe that most of us make both bad and good decisions in life.
The important thing is that we learn from the bad and try to turn them into good.
However, you reap what you sow...

What you put all your energy into in this life will have an everlasting impact on what you will get out of it.

I feel the need to share with you that I had to rewrite this chapter because when I originally wrote it, I was very angry and upset. I got very depressed on the day I was writing this chapter and had to wait a whole week to try writing it again. To be honest, I am not exactly sure why. I am still healing, and I believe I will be trying to heal for the rest of my life. I know this chapter was important for me to write because it stood out in my mind, and it really bothered me. I guess it just felt like they just ended.
It made me feel like they did not have any generations left

even though all 4 of their children were still alive and we all have children. As I sit here thinking about that estate sale, I have this empty feeling mixed with sadness for both of them. Although they had many material possessions and money in this life, they ended up being the poorest people I ever knew.

If I could leave you with one last thought...

Put God first in your life and focus your love and attention on those that God has given you to love.
You will become far richer than you ever thought possible.

CHAPTER 32
Ruth

On 12/27/2019 I received a text from a childhood friend that lived in the neighborhood a block away from me growing up. She wanted to get together and have coffee but before we were able to get together Covid happened, so we had to cancel. Ruth contacted me again on March 18th, 2023, to try to get together and so we set up a new day to get together which was on May 16th, 2023 (Ruth picked the date.)

On Thursday, May 11th, 2023, my sister Mila, and I decided that she would help me finish writing my book and that we would partner in starting a non-profit business to help others that are dealing with different kinds of abuse and trauma and help them tell their story either by helping them write their story and/or by sharing it.

On Monday May 15th, 2023, Mila and I started our very first day planning our new venture for God.
While we were working, I received a text from Ruth telling me she may have only an hour to meet with me the following day because she needed to take her mother-in-law to a doctor's appointment. I had a feeling

that she was going to cancel but I told her that an
hour was fine.

The next morning when I was driving on the way to meet
Ruth, I had a sense that she was nervous.

When I walked into the coffee shop, my old friend was
there waiting for me. We caught up on the basics of
the usual things old friends talk about after not seeing
one another in over two decades, and then Ruth said
something that surprised me. She said that she wished
both of my parents were still alive. She told me that
going to my house for dinner or the occasional sleep
over were some of the happiest memories she had
as a child.

You might find this odd, but I was genuinely filled with
a sense of peace and an unexpected joy to see her so
happy talking about my parents.

I knew at that moment that I had to share the secret I
had kept for so many years with her because if I didn't, I
would feel like I was lying to her.

I told her how happy I was that spending time at my
house growing up was a good thing for her. However, I
told her that it was not the same for me. I proceeded to
tell her about the abuse that I endured from my father
and Ruth was shocked and saddened to hear what I
told her. As Ruth's eyes filled with tears, I told her not
to be sad because I wasn't sad. I knew now that I went
through everything I went through for a reason and
that I was going to take all the pain and yuck and use it
to help others and lead people to God. I told her about
the book that I had been writing for the past 21 years
and about the non-profit company that Mila and I were

starting. I told her how Mila, my husband and I had been under attack from the evil one (In case you don't know what I mean by that, I will explain).

When you are doing good things in your life to help people or trying to do good in this world, there is evil in this world that will attack you and go after the weaknesses in your life so that you stop doing good. Ruth told me how she almost canceled the day before and how she normally doesn't ever get nervous because she has always been very outspoken and confident (she has always been that way since we were little girls, and I was the exact opposite) but she said for some reason that she was getting really nervous and anxious the morning that we met which is extremely out of character for her. I believe that the devil was trying to stop us from getting together.

Ruth is a strong woman of faith on fire for The Lord. I am sure the evil in this world did not want us joining forces and rekindling our friendship. Ruth proceeded to ask me if I would be interested in speaking on her friend's podcast. I told her yes, but not until I was done writing my book and we had moved further along with the non-profit. I told her how terrified I was about speaking in public but that I knew that I was going to speak in front of people since I was in the 5th grade. I told her that when I was in 5th grade, we had to make a speech in front of the class but when the teacher called my name, I wouldn't go up to do it. The teacher told me in front of the whole class that she was going to give me an "F." I said OK and left the classroom to go to the bathroom to cry. When I was on the way to the bathroom, I heard this small voice inside me tell me that I was going to be speaking in front of many people one day. I remember that I started arguing with that voice in my head and saying, "There is no way in hell that I am going to do that! The same small voice told me, "Wait and see." I told Ruth about the many dreams I had throughout my life since I was in the 5th grade where I was on a stage in front of a lot of people speaking.

To be honest, for many years of my life they were like nightmares to me because of my fear of attention and feeling like I didn't have anything important to say. I have known in the back of my mind through every job, career, volunteer work and basically through everything I have gone through that God was preparing me for something having to do with speaking in front of people. I have learned in my life and through stories in the bible that the greatest works God uses us for is not with the greatest gifts that we possess but with our greatest fears and weaknesses.

Ruth told me that if I do a podcast that I wouldn't have to speak in front of people. I told her that I knew that God wanted me to speak in front of people, so I had to. I told her that I wasn't going to think about speaking in front of people now, that I was just going to finish writing this book and that God would use me when he was ready.

When I went to meet Mila later that day, I told her about Ruth asking me about being a guest on her friend's podcast and she told me that she hadn't wanted to scare me or stress me out before I finished writing my book but that she wanted to talk to me about doing a podcast for our non-profit. I told Mila that I was open to doing whatever God led us to do.

After meeting Ruth, for the first time I realized I was filled with a peaceful joy knowing that somehow Ruth felt a reprieve from her home life. Her parents were divorced when Ruth was young. Ruth was the eldest of three children and she took care of both of her siblings. They all lived with her mom who was an alcoholic and rarely home.

Both of my parents really liked Ruth, she was always outgoing, outspoken, and always showed such huge appreciation for everything, including my mom's cooking.

Ruth looked up to both of my parents and my father loved how she looked up to him. I told Ruth that my father never hurt me when she was at our house so the nights, she slept over at our house were a blessing to me.

Ruth ended up telling me that morning that we met, that she remembered a few times when we were little kids, that I told her that I wanted to tell her something, but it was a secret, and I couldn't tell her. She told me that as we got older, I told her that same thing a few other times. She told me that she never asked me about what it was because she could tell that I didn't want her to ask.

I am so thankful for getting reunited with my old friend and I am grateful to God for giving me the strength to voice my truth to her. I have learned the hard way that we were not meant to be alone in our pain and we were not meant to be keeping secrets that were not meant for us to keep.

I also learned from meeting with Ruth that even in the darkest places God can shed light into someone's life.
I am happy to find some goodness in the most unlikely of places. I received a special healing when I found out that good came from my abusive home.

May God guide you out of your darkness and into the light of his faithful love.

CHAPTER 33

Conclusion

God used many people and many prayers to get me to the place he knew where ultimately, I would find the deep healing, he wanted for me. I can honestly say now that I am writing my last chapter of this book that I did need to finish my story to receive ultimate healing. Now that I realize why I needed to finish this book I have grown spiritually stronger than ever before. I have a purpose that is not about me, it is about you and most importantly, it is about God.

I struggled for so many years trying to finish writing this book, but the same fear kept shouting at me which made me stop time and time again. The voice I heard was telling me that I was a nobody, and no one would care about anything that I wrote, especially about my life. That awful voice in my head was the devil.
I also realize that I am a nobody, but God always uses nobody's like me because he is God, and he makes nobody's like me into somebody's.

I first started writing this book so that my kids would understand me better after hearing about all that I had gone through. I wanted them to understand why I was the way I was with all my quirks and maybe if they got a glimpse of me through my story, I would make more sense to them. I had planned on leaving it for them after I died because I never wanted them to know what happened to me because I was ashamed, embarrassed, and felt so dirty. However, I ended up telling my kids about my life many years ago because I felt like I was lying to them, and I didn't want anything to keep us from being as close as we could be. It was a very difficult thing for me to do but I know that it was the right decision.

Right after I started writing my book, I realized that maybe I could help people by sharing my story. For other people that felt as lonely as I did, for those that felt depressed, lost, angry, hurt, sad and forgotten. That is what has pushed me to keep on trying to write.
This road has obviously been extremely difficult for me, otherwise it wouldn't have taken 21 years and my closest friend to finally help me finish writing it.

I want you to know that I am a very happily married woman now with 5 grown children that I share with my husband of over 10 years of marriage. My life and my heart are both filled with love and joy.

For those of you that have been abused and broken in any way and feel any of the feelings I have mentioned in this book, I want you to know it is so important for you to tell your story whether it is verbally or written. There is a special healing that is waiting for you when you write about the pain and you overcoming it, even if it is for your eyes only.

I am not afraid anymore; I am not embarrassed or ashamed by what I have gone through because I found a purpose for all the yuck that happened to me in my life. My purpose is to help you to stop keeping your secrets and for you to understand that it wasn't your fault, just like it wasn't my fault. I know the road to healing is not easy, but I do know that it is worth it. Please remember that you are not alone, so many of us have been abused and broken but most of us do not speak out about it. Maybe if we start speaking out about it then we can help heal others earlier in their lives. Writing and reading what I wrote repeatedly made me realize how far I have come with so many painful challenges I went through in my life. I realize that every hardship I went through taught me a lesson that I grew from. Even in the many mistakes I have made in my life, I realize now that they also helped me to become the person I am today.

This book was not about the story of my life, although I needed to tell it for you to understand about the depth of forgiveness that is there for all of us. This book is about the true healing of absolute forgiveness despite the depth of pain and hurt we are in.

In this book I walked you through the journey of my life to show proof that it is possible to heal and forgive even when our world we live in shows so many reasons why we shouldn't.

When God has plans for healing, there is no stopping him. I pray that God finds you right where you are, in whatever pain you are in and whatever pain you may have caused.

There is healing and forgiveness for each one of us, despite how deep the pain runs.

I will end this book with the one scripture that helped me through the hardest times of my life.

**I can do all things through Christ who strengthens me.
—Philippians 4:13**

Letter of Acknowledgement

I wouldn't have been able to complete this book without the help of two very important people …

My amazing and loving husband, whose love, support, and encouragement were instrumental in helping me achieve my lifelong goal of finishing my book.

My Sister in Christ, my person…whose commitment to helping me finish this book never faltered. Her faith in me never wavered. She helped me find the healing I needed by keeping me focused and grounded on finishing it. I honestly could not have finished my book without you.

I love you both very much.

A WORD FROM THE AUTHOR ABOUT
Voice Your Truth Ministries

Voice your Truth Ministries was started in the hopes of helping other people that have been victims of abuse.

After the struggle of completing my book that took me 21 years to write, the amount of healing that I received was so substantial that I was moved to do more...
so I decided to help others achieve the ultimate healing of helping them to write, publish and tell their stories.

By sharing about our pain, our loneliness, our shame and our "Secrets," I found that there is a special healing and emotional empowerment at the end of our journey of telling our truth or in my case writing my truth and sharing my testimony.

The Religious Non-Profit Voice Your Truth Ministries' specific purpose is to guide individuals to have a deeper relationship with God by writing our stories, sharing our testimonies and helping others to do the same.

For more information, please go to:
www.VoiceYourTruthMinistries.com

www.ingramcontent.com/pod-product-compliance
Lightning Source LLC
Chambersburg PA
CBHW051613120626
46551CB00014B/1780